# THE AGONIZED HEART...
## No More

*Abandon Abusers*

# LINDA LOU JONES

I0078868

*** Special thanks to Janice Pearson, for her editorial assistance. ***

Copyright © 2013 Linda Lou Jones
All rights reserved.
ISBN: 0980892902
ISBN 13: 9780980892901

Unless otherwise indicated all Scripture quotations are taken from the
King James Version of the Bible.

All publishing rights belong exclusively to Rainbow Revelations
Published By: RainbowRevelations In Canada
Publisher/Editor: Linda Lou Jones
Assistant Editor: Janice Pearson

*Some names and identifying details have been changed
to protect the privacy of individuals and their families.

Printed in the United States of America. All rights reserved under International
Copyright Law. Contents and/or cover may not be reproduced in whole or in part in any
form without the express written consent of the publisher.
Website: www.LindaLouJones.com
e-Book: The Rent Is Paid
Blog: https://www.rightlady.blogspot.com
Follow Me On Twitter: https://www.twitter.com/rightlady7

# TABLE OF CONTENTS

# DEDICATION

I Dedicate This Book To
**JESUS CHRIST**
My Best Friend & Much More

Thank You
For Revealing Yourself To Me
So Many Times
As The Holy Spirit Led Me
Through The Fiery Furnace Successfully!

You Inspired Hope
Replaced Fear With Faith
Death With Life
Flooded Me With Love
Peace Became My Umpire
And Joy Strengthened Me

Thank You
For Instructing Me
To Write This Book
That Others May Receive Help
As Did I
I Am FREE

*Linda Lou Jones*

**John 8:36 "If the Son therefore
Shall make you free, ye shall be free indeed."**

# WHY I WROTE THIS BOOK:

THERE ARE MANY PEOPLE WITH A hidden area of their life that needs to be exposed with truth. I was one of them. The hidden area was the fact that I was a victim of domestic abuse. Furthermore, my husband and I were both Christians, Spirit filled tongue speaking believers snared. One of us was the bully. One of us was the enabler. Product produced ... victims with agonized hearts. Hell on earth resulted.

Bottom line: I want others to be set free so they can become the person God created them to be. Never live in fear again. Chapter one tells how I felt physically when God spoke to me and asked me to write this book. I did not want to do it. In fact, I declined; knowing to write it meant I had to relive everything. I had no intention of going through that again.

But God knows how to ask one question that resulted in my change of minset. I did what He asked me to do and started to write. It was a huge turning point in my life although I did not realize it at the time. Now that I am free and have stayed free for over a decade, it is time to reveal the keys to my success because there are many victims that need help. God know who they are and wants to help them. Silence is not the answer.

If you are not a victim, you may know someone who is. This is your opportunity to learn how to identify such a person, as well as help stop the abuse of an adult or a child. It will be easier for you to read than it was for me to live it, let alone write it. Walk with me through each page as if entering a fiery furnace. Because hell is hot and void of peace, as was my life... for far too long! No more though...no more!

I learned that a victim must first come out of denial and deception before becoming a deliver for other victims. It is transformation time. Change begins in your heart as you read, accept and apply truth. The decision is yours.

Jesus is coming for a Bride without spot or wrinkle. Abused Christians are wounded warriors whose effectiveness for the Kingdom of God is hindered.

I invite you to step into the furnace, the fiery furnace and read each page. Preparation proceeds promotion. Remember, when Jesus asks us to do something it is not without a purpose. Trusting him is the right thing to do. Jesus simply, sincerely, and lovingly says, **"Come."**

# 1. CHALLENGE ACCEPTED

God, the porcupine quills
Are hurting so much
From inside
Pushing tears out
As I have cried and cried

I accept your challenge
To write a book on abuse
So You can set people free
Including me
'Cause I know You'll heal me
As I write from my heart each day
I'll complete it in less than one year

It will cause many to shed tears
As the Holy Ghost heals them too
Sets them free from cocoons of deception
Heals their mind, will, emotions

Causes them to be free
Free to smile
Free to laugh again
Free to be loved
Free to help others
Get free

GLORY TO GOD

# 2. EXPOSING ABUSE

FIVE MONTHS AFTER DIVORCING MY HUSBAND of sixteen years for mental and emotional cruelty, I became a sincere and dedicated Christian. For thirteen more years I was a single parent. Then, when my two children were grown and married, I married a second time. My husband Clint and I were both born again Christians, but after a decade of marriage it looked like there would be a divorce. I was in an abusive relationship again. This is the story of that second marriage and how God brought me through.

Did I know about praying and breaking generational curses? Yes, I did. Then why did I allow the mental, emotional and physical abuse to continue for so many years? Why did I bury the incidents deep in my heart rather than face them? Burying them was my first reaction. You'll see as you read along, it took a real work of God's grace to bring me to a place of peace and joy and safety.

The first incident of abuse with Clint occurred when we were married nearly one year. I was concerned about something, so I went into the living room to talk it over with him. His response was to slap me across the face. I was astounded and stunned—absolutely devastated. Perhaps even moreso because he showed no remorse. None.

The next incident occurred a few months later when we were moving. Clint was from Texas, USA and I was from Ontario, Canada. Clint drove a rental truck pulling our pickup on a trailer, and I followed in our car. We stayed overnight at a motel. I do not remember what we were talking about, but I do remember it was in the morning when we were dressed and nearly ready to leave the room.

He suddenly grabbed me by the neck with both hands and started choking me. He let me go when my shoulder bumped the wall, probably because he feared someone in the next room would hear and might call for help.

I fell to the floor and caught my breath. When I looked up he was turned away and heading out the door. He showed no remorse, absolutely none. I was in shock. Here I was, moving sixteen hundred miles away from my home in Ontario, Canada to please my husband, and this was happening.

I was not in a position to turn the car around, abandon everything and head back to Canada. I could not even think straight. I felt like a robot as I got in the car and followed him down that highway, tears streaming down my face and my heart broken. I had never in my life suffered such physical abuse. Although there had been abuse in my first marriage, my first husband had never, ever slapped me. This was a shock.

Time passed, and one morning six months after moving to Texas it happened again. He grabbed me by the throat and started to squeeze. I was absolutely helpless. At 5'6" and 150 pounds I was no match for his 6'1½" and 250 pounds.

In my heart I cried out to God but no words came out of my mouth. The pain was unlike anything I had experienced before. Again, he let go suddenly and started heading out of the room. I am convinced that somewhere, someone was interceding for me.

I then heard these words come out of my mouth, *"You have a mental problem!"* He looked at me over his shoulder as he was leaving the room, and I saw the fear in his eyes. I knew I had hit the nail on the head. But now what?

I knew he was on medication for what he had told me was a chemical imbalance. He had told me about it before we were married, but he said that God had healed him and he no longer suffered from depression.

I believed him and did not condemn him. He was ill but was getting help. Before long, though, I knew he had not told me the truth. I started to see a pattern unfold.

Clint drove an eighteen-wheeler and would be away several days at a time. We had agreed that he would call me each evening. After a while, I began to notice that he was avoiding phoning me. He would tell me he was busy loading or unloading the truck and couldn't call; he fell asleep and forgot to call; he was upset about something and didn't want to talk. Or, he would call me when he knew I would be out and leave a message on the answering machine.

So I got smart and turned the answering machine off! I wanted to speak with my husband directly. I guess what I really wanted was the kind of marriage where we were best friends and would want to talk to each other. That's God's plan for marriage, and that's what I was longing for!

So why didn't he want to talk with me? I had to face the fact that there was unforgiveness in his heart. Otherwise, why wouldn't he call? In fact, it was becoming clearer to me as time progressed that he had a huge problem forgiving anything or anyone. I could not figure out the reason, but I knew it was very deep.

I tried to outsmart him by turning off the answering machine, but I soon realized that he was outsmarting me! He would call when he knew I would not be home and let the phone ring ten times, knowing that would turn the answering machine on automatically. Then he would leave a message. This seemed to really thrill him. I knew he took it as a great victory when he made contact without talking to me personally. It was sick.

It hurt. I was frustrated and could not understand why he would not talk to me. He was like a little kid playing games and manipulating, yet he was a grown man. I did not know what to do. Whenever he returned home from work I never knew what kind of mood he would be in.

He was always very tired and worn out, for sure. I understood, given the miles that a long haul driver puts in, but I could not understand his anger over little incidents. He consistently made mountains out of molehills. I learned to walk on eggshells in an effort not to make him angry, yet I was not responsible for his anger.

Tension grew. Stress increased. Fear mounted. Some of it was subconscious because I really did not realize how much his anger was affecting me. Not to mention how the abuse was affecting me. I was in much denial.

# 3. NORTH MEETS SOUTH

MY HEART IS FREELY RELEASING THE words that my fingers are typing because there are no notes to refer to, simply instant recall as the Holy Spirit brings to me what needs to be shared with you. My trust is in God to stir up the writing gift He gave me and cause it to be used for His glory and to help many people.

It could be that you have never been in an abusive relationship. Thank God for that, but you may know someone who is being abused. As you read this book God will reveal things to you that will help you recognize red flags in the lives of others who do need help. As a result, you can reach out to be a lifeline to them, so don't limit God by saying, *"I can't relate to abuse."* Open your heart and receive more knowledge; He will show you how to apply that knowledge as time goes on.

This was a second marriage for both Clint and me. His first wife had died of cancer one year before he and I met. His two children were grown and married, as were mine.

As for me, my first marriage ended in divorce after sixteen years. I divorced my husband because of mental and emotional abuse, the most difficult grounds on which to get a divorce back then.

Five months after the divorce, I became a committed Christian. For the next thirteen years I prayed for God to send me the right Christian husband. (By then my children were married.) **I prayed God would bring him to me and do it in such a way that I would know without a doubt that he was the one for me. God did exactly that.**

God had told me I would marry an American, and that I would live in the United States. I had written some poems about Texas, although I had never been there. Little did I know when I wrote them that I would end up living there for many years. But I'm getting ahead of myself ... I guess now is the best time to let you know how Clint and I met.

For the third consecutive summer I was singing at a mobile chapel that came to my town in Ontario. It was owned and run by a couple that travelled across the USA and into Ontario. They would stop at various truck stops en route to their destinations and evangelize the truckers and their families who attended their services. They had been doing this for several years. Each night of the week that they were in my area I would sing and pray with the drivers.

One night the chaplain's wife called me into their living quarters at the end of the service. This was a first, and it concerned me because I thought that maybe I had done something out of order. I did not ever want that to happen. We sat across from each other and she said, "*My husband and I have met someone. He's a trucker, long haul, loves the Lord.*"

As she looked directly into my eyes, I thought to myself, "*They are always meeting people. What is she saying? Lord, is she working too hard; has she lost it? They meet people all the time.*"

Then she said, "*He's a widower.*" She paused and continued to look at me. I looked right back at her, and when I got the picture I thought, "**Is SHE matchmaking?!!! I don't need some woman to pick a guy out for me. I can do that myself!**" I was quite indignant about it.

She continued to stare right through me, or so it seemed. I mustered up enough courage to ask, "*Children?*" I was concerned because I knew I would not be raising any more children or having any more, since that is what the Lord had impressed on me some time before. So this was an important question. She said, "*Two, grown.*" I thought "*Whew!*" I asked, "*What's his name?*" She answered, "*Clint Smith.*"

I know my eyes popped then, because Jones is my surname. Talk about God having a sense of humor! We both smiled and it kind of broke the tension, because this was intense.

I thought to myself that they must have met him when they crossed the border, maybe at the truck stop in Milton, Ontario, or in Niagara Falls. So I asked, "*Where does he live?*" She said, "*Texas!*" "**TEXAS!!!**" I exclaimed. My heart sank and I had to fight off some anger because I felt like she had set me up. To learn he lived in Texas was shocking. Texas is 1600 miles away!!! How do you date someone that far away?!!! I had mixed emotions indeed.

Then she said, "*My husband and I would like to give him this video of you singing, if that is okay with you.*" The wheels were turning in my head and I thought to myself, "*Well, that must mean she thinks we'd be a good match or she wouldn't do this.*"

So, long story short, I gave my permission. I included a music cassette I recorded of some of my songs from earlier years and a photo of myself. Then I went home and waited for a phone call. I knew drivers didn't have time to write letters or even to phone. My brother drove long haul for years, so I was not a total greenhorn to the trucking industry and its perils.

Time passed and the phone call did not come. One evening I said, "*Lord, that is not the guy for me. He is not even appreciative enough to call and say thank you for the cassette, even if he is not interested in me; so I just throw him on the altar and you can have him. He's not for me.*"

Much to my amazement, the very next day the phone rang and I was introduced to Clint Jones by the chaplain. I nearly dropped the phone. We talked for an hour, and it was as if we had known each other all of our lives.

He had just arrived at the truck stop where the chaplains were ministering near Chicago. He watched the video, and then we were introduced. He was a fifth generation Texan so he had quite a strong Texas accent, which was very endearing.

Near the end of the conversation he said in a slow drawl, "*Well ah'd sure like to call you again sometime Ma'am, if that's okay?*" I said, "*That's fine.*" Two days later he called and we talked for **15 ½ hours!** (That is not a typing error.) The bill was $242.00.

We talked about everything you talk about when you are getting to know someone. God supernaturally caught both of us up, so what would have taken a year or so to learn about each other took one telephone conversation, albeit a long one!

He was at a motel and the clerk thought something was wrong with the phone because the light was on so long, so she disconnected us. We reconnected until God was done what He was doing. Clint called daily for about six weeks. Sometimes we talked one hour, or three, or even five hours. Both of us were hesitant because we both questioned how to work out dating. But **God had a plan.**

During one of our phone conversations I shocked myself when I heard myself ask, completely unplanned, *"So, when are you coming to Canada?"* He answered that he had never been to Canada. Later he told me he knew right then that he would be coming here. Soon thereafter he parked his truck, locked up everything, and drove to Canada in his car for the first time.

I had a few friends who knew about these conversations and were praying. One of my friends was with me at the chapel the night the chaplain called me in, so she knew all the details. She would call me from work asking, *"Did he phone last night? What did he say?"* We would laugh and I would try to sound like I had a Texas accent because I liked it.

Then one day she burst into tears on the phone. I was so surprised and asked what was wrong. She said, *"It's just that it brings so much glory to God."* And she wept some more. That really touched my heart. Then a relatively new acquaintance from church called when she learned Clint was coming to Canada.

She asked me where he would be staying. I answered, *"Well, not here!"* Then she explained she had talked to her boyfriend who was a widower and who lived two miles from me. On weekends he would go to his lake home. He offered to let Clint stay at his home as long as he was going to be in Canada. THAT is when I got scared.

I hardly knew this woman and had only met her boyfriend once, but I was seeing doors opening fast. I recognized God's hand of provision. Then my friend asked if I had a video camera. I did not. She said she was coming to give me a crash course on using hers and that I could use it when Clint and I met. So I agreed.

When Clint crossed the border he was not too happy, as the customs officials searched his car thoroughly. He said it seemed to him that the law thinks everyone from Texas has a gun! Anyway, we made arrangements to meet at the truck stop where I made the video.

I must interject now and tell you that I am writing these details so that you will understand how God put my husband and me together and that we truly were God's choice for each other. Just because it ended in divorce does not mean we were not to marry. It means there was hardness of heart. Sometimes we have to go through the valley, but as I learned, I was never alone. For all that He did, God gets all the glory.

I am writing this book in obedience to the Holy Spirit's instruction. Even though the marriage failed miserably, this book WILL bring glory to God, and that makes me very happy indeed. I paid my dues and will now see good come out of it all. Nothing we go through is ever in vain when we stay focused on the Lord Jesus Christ. Nothing! Okay, back to the rendezvous at the truck stop.

One friend picked me up. Another friend came also, carrying a bouquet of beautiful fresh cut flowers. I was wondering why she had them. We drove to the truck stop where Clint and I had arranged to meet.

I had asked Clint how I would recognize him. He said, *"I will be wearing jeans, a western shirt, and western boots."* I told him, *"So will every other trucker!"* He described his car and I said we would meet him at the front entrance. Then he said, *"I will say, Hi Darlin', I'm Clint."*

Little did we three women know Clint had phoned me from a different town than the one we had agreed upon, which meant it took less time than we had planned for him to get there. So he arrived before us, only to discover we were not waiting at the front entrance. We were nowhere to be found.

I had told him there would be three women meeting him. He searched the restaurant and store but found no one. He thought he had been stood up after driving 1600 miles! Not a good feeling. I can guarantee you his cheeks were very red, so he looked like the blushing groom. It wasn't shyness though. He was pretty angry and disappointed because of what he was thinking.

Finally, though, we drove in and spotted his car right away. I saw him standing at the steps, very tall, and knew it was him. As we approached him we must have looked like tourists—I had a little camera around my neck, one friend had the flowers, and the other friend had the movie camera. I wore a white cotton eyelet dress with touches of pink trim and white heels. When I got to the steps I looked up and stopped at the bottom step. I just couldn't go any further. My heart was in my mouth.

Then he said, with a twinkle in his eye, *"Hi Darlin', I'm Clint."* We embraced, and as we turned I was handed the flowers. I was so surprised. Talk about perfect timing. We all went inside and had breakfast. To this day I cannot remember what I ate, or even if I ate. We talked and laughed and had such a great time.

Then we went outside and I got in his car, somewhat timidly. It was a big step. We drove about 10 miles to my friend's home where Clint would stay while visiting Canada. My apartment was a few miles from there. We met friends of mine and went to a restaurant for dinner. After dinner we drove to Lake Ontario and took a long walk along the waterfront.

On the second day I had an engagement ring, and eleven days later we were en route to the USA to meet the chaplains at their mobile chapel. We planned to be married in that chapel, the same one in which the movie was made of me singing. (After we were married I was told about a vision the chaplain had of Clint and me being married. She did not tell us before we were married. This is why she made the video of me singing, as a point of contact to get us together.)

As I look back, I see the hand of God in all the details of our wedding. He is the perfect wedding planner, and He has a really good eye for fashion! Sometime earlier I had bought a new pair of high heels but had never gotten around to wearing them. I wasn't sure why I hadn't worn them, but I found out. I was saving them for my wedding day!

As Clint and I drove from Ontario to the United States, we stopped to eat and I found a pretty clip with dangling pearls to wear in my hair, so I bought it. When we arrived at our destination, Clint took me to a large store selling wedding gowns and told me to buy whichever dress I wanted, have it boxed up, then he would come in and pay for it.

The huge signs on the window said 70% off, closing sale. This was the favor of God. Immediately I found the perfect dress. It fit perfectly, and the deal was made. The clerks were all excited as I shared my testimony. I told them I had been single for thirteen years and prayed that if God had someone for me, He would bring him to me in such a way that I would know without a doubt that he was the one. And He did!

Details simply clicked together magnificently. My high heeled leather shoes with a perfect rose above the toes were from Ontario; my hair decoration was from Indiana; the wedding dress was from Wyoming, and they all matched perfectly! God put it all together!! (If anyone knows how to be a good wedding planner, He does. He's been doing it for generations and He is still preparing His Bride!)

I had never met my hairstylist before, but she did a great job too. Our blood work (in the USA a couple needs to get a blood test before they can marry) was done without delay. Neither one of us had any family there in Wyoming, but we knew God was there, along with people from the family of God.

We were getting married in the chapel that was parked at a truck stop. For those who are not familiar with the trucking industry, the trailer of an 18wheeler is the actual chapel. Inside it is professionally decorated, walls panelled, seats on each side, a pulpit at one end, center aisle, possible holds twenty or more people. The chapel was decorated beautifully, as was the truckers' lounge at the large truck stop where the chapel was parked. The chef baked us a wedding cake, and **God put a rainbow in the sky that day,** then some rain, then sunshine. 'Rainbow' was my nickname for decades after using citizens band radio. Also, *Rainbow's Breakin' Thru* was the title of a song I wrote and recorded years earlier, on cassette. So it all meant a lot at the time. I walked three short steps down the chapel aisle (remember, it was in a trailer) and we were married while I sang ... via my music cassette that played in the background.

A reporter from the local newspaper came and interviewed us and put our picture on the front page of the paper the next day. We hit the news on TV, and one of the chaplains was interviewed.

Two days later the reporter returned to the truck stop and gave us the rolls of film he had taken. God even provided a photographer! He looked after every detail magnificently. After all, when you get married eleven days after you meet, over a thousand miles from home in another country, it is not like you have time to do much planning. But God had a plan, and He used people to bring it all to pass.

After we were married Clint told me when he watched the video of me singing, God spoke to him. He said, **"This is the woman I have for you as a wife."** I said, "*What did you do then?*" He said, **"I watched it four times!"** ☺

We stayed at the truck stop motel and fellowshipped with the chaplains for a few days. Then we drove to meet Clint's family in Texas. I was a bit nervous, but they were happy for him and it all worked out fine. I felt kind of like a 'novelty' under everyone's scrutiny and looked forward to getting back in the truck and getting out on the big road.

# 4. WITHOUT TRUCKS ... AMERICA STOPS!

WE MOVED CLINT'S MOBILE HOME OUT of state and lived away from both our families for one year. I sang at various truck stops as we trucked down the big road. Doors were always open and the drivers—male and female—and their families, were appreciative.

Our eighteen wheeler was unlike most because the back doors of the trailer were painted with scripture in red lettering: *John 3:16 "For God so loved the world, that he gave his only begotten Son, that whosoever believeth in him should not perish, but have everlasting life."* The cab had three red crosses on each side of the sleeper, plus "Jesus Is Lord".

The white mud flaps on the trailer had the words in red: **"ONLY JESUS SAVES."** Many times, as we drove down the highway at night drivers behind us commented on the scripture ... favorably too! I did a lot of ministering and singing on the CB radio as we drove across country and back, often hauling beef from Texas to Chicago.

Clint drove a flatbed truck hauling steel, a refrigerated unit (reefer) hauling produce, and he hauled hazardous chemicals. During the first two years we were married, the Lord gave me quite a few songs for truckers. When I went on the truck with my husband, we would not be on the interstate ten minutes before God would give me a new song.

I would get out of the jump seat and go into the bunk area, set up my tape recorder and microphone, take pen and paper and let the Holy Spirit flow. It was awesome. He gave me compassion for the drivers and their families. I knew the sacrifice they all made and I wrote about it. Being a long-haul trucker requires much sacrifice by the entire trucker family, but it's necessary because, as you may have heard, **"Without Trucks, America Stops!"**

God revealed His viewpoint, and through the lyrics He gave me, drivers were uplifted as they realized that God saw them. He saw these tired drivers press on for that final fifty mile stretch at 4 a.m. so they could get the load delivered in time. God saw the out-of-season groceries being made available to customers—fruit such as fresh strawberries and watermelons made it to the stores because a driver drove all night! People seldom thought about how those groceries got to their supermarket shelves, or the sacrifices that were made to get them there, but God knew.

Lives were literally risked at times when roads were bad, icy, foggy and crowded from construction and summer traffic, yet the wheels kept turning. Whether the driver was hauling cattle to the butcher, or frozen beef in a reefer to the store, you can be sure the drivers sacrificed sleep and a lot more. That's their life.

It is their job, yes, but how does your heart respond when someone lets you know that your labor is appreciated? It does something to you, doesn't it? It makes you feel worthwhile when someone lets you know they did not take it for granted that you sacrificed like you did, worked when your body wanted to sleep, delivered the goods when other families were celebrating Christmas Eve and other holidays together. Everyone likes to be appreciated!

Although my husband and I were not without some serious problems, I was clearly able to see strong points in him. He loved trucking—long haul— and had no desire to do any other kind of job whatsoever. That was his passion. It was reflected in his performance—he would do paperwork diligently at all hours, sitting on the bunk, barely able to keep his eyes open. He took pride in keeping the truck in good condition, not to mention delivering the load on time. He was never late! Even in ice storms there was no stopping him. Some of these memories inspired me to create this poem to honor him on his birthday:

# A DONE DEAL

Your heart is hid
To but very few
Yet I am still
In love with you.
A man who is near
To God's heart and Word.
A man whose heart
Few have really heard.

Yet God sees and knows
All you say, think, and do
And for your good work
He will abundantly bless you.
He knows the number of miles
You have driven to meet a need
Delivering your load as unto Him
Enabling others to feed

They received what they needed
Everything from grain to vegetables to beef
Clothing, milk, ice cream
The loads brought much relief
The recipient did not necessarily know
This driver drove all night long
While he or she was home sleeping
He delivered on time, right or wrong

'Cause to deliver on time
Often meant backing up a log book

To accommodate the need
Yet praying the D.O.T. would not look

If it had been delivered
With log book A+
The load would not be on time
And this, you've never done

You've taken pride in your career
Whilst some condemned you
How wonderful to know you have fulfilled
What God called you to do

I respect and love you
For pressing on year after year
Whether we are together or miles apart
We are still near

'Cause our love is Christ centered
And we pray God's will be done
Happy Birthday Clint
Congratulations on a job
Well Done
Even delivering steel … and now
It's a DONE DEAL!!!

Written By Your Wife, 1998

So the Lord used me and my husband to minister to those drivers—those men and women—and to their families. He gave me many opportunities to minister the Word of God on the CB radio, and I received a lot of positive feedback from many of the drivers.

I seldom got to see their faces but I could feel their hearts and knew they were sincere. There is no distance in the spirit. Each encounter was a Divine appointment. God put His words in my mouth whether I was sharing testimony of His faithfulness, reading a poem He had given me, singing songs, or praying with and for them.

I remember all the hours and hours on end of praying in the Spirit as the wheels turned. I would get built up and ready for the next round of ministering to others or to my husband, regardless of the time.

As I would minister, the words would flow. One man came back on the CB radio and said, *"I want you to know Oral Roberts doesn't have anything on you. You are just as good as he is. You keep up the good work; this is wonderful!"* I had to grin, but I did tell him that the same Spirit who gives Oral Roberts the words gives me the words, so I cannot take any credit. God gets all the glory.

Then there were other times when I would get so angry as drivers were convicted of sin but would not want to change. They did not want to be free. Instead, they chose to be involved with prostitutes, homosexuals, and other sins and perversions.

I remember telling one man who was soliciting for another man on the radio that there is nothing he has done that will make Jesus Christ stop loving him because HE doesn't change! This fellow just about came unglued from conviction and rebellion. He keyed that mike and shouted, *"Where are you at?"* He didn't find me, but God found his heart and brought conviction. It was awesome.

I recall drivers asking me to sing *Amazing Grace* over and over again. It was absolutely their favorite hymn. I sang country Gospel songs most of the time. I also sold cassettes of some of my songs to individual drivers by Divine appointment.

So for eleven years we were married. But just because both the husband and the wife are born again, Spirit-filled Christians, it does not guarantee instant success and a problem-free life. Christians who are serving God are a threat to the devil, and he attacks. I have told you about how we met and married, and the joys of our life and ministry together on the road. But now it is time to tell the other side of the story.

I need to explain something before I go on. Writing this book was not my idea. In fact, when the Holy Spirit asked me to write it, I said a quick "*No.*" I was horrified at the thought of having to relive all that pain. I knew I would have to relive it in order to write about it, and I had absolutely no desire whatsoever to face it all again. BUT GOD ... has a way of changing hearts. First the Holy Spirit asked me to go to a Christian bookstore and let Him know what books I found that He could use to help people come out of abuse.

The thought kind of intrigued me, so I said, "*Okay, I will!*" Mind you, I was thinking there would be several, so that would let me off the hook so to speak. Well, I drove seven miles to the largest bookstore and found only two books. One of them fell kind of flat, and the other did have some light regarding emotional abuse. My heart was wrenched when I realized the void.

Obviously, God knew too because He sent me there. I was in tears before I got out of the store, and I cried all the way home, knowing I had to write the book. There really was no option. It was a turning point that helped me ... far more than I realized it would. When God gets a point across, He doesn't mess around. Done deal! I wrote as I received healings from Him, so it is not in chronological order. To change it would not present a true picture. Stress caused fragmentation. **God helped me pick up the pieces, mentally ... one at a time. I wrote as healings were received. What I lived, I wrote ... from the bottom of a very broken heart ... until it was healed.**

Now it is time to move down the abuse road since my heart is finally ready to release all of it. I realize that the sooner I get it out, the sooner I will be healed.

# 5. FACING DEATH ON THE ROAD

As I SHARE WITH YOU, WOUNDS are opened in my spirit. Then God cleanses the wounds, fills them with love, and makes me stronger than ever before in those areas as He works all things together for good (*Romans 8:28*). It is one of my favorite scriptures because I know that I know God can make good come out of anything—absolutely anything.

This does not mean that He wants unfortunate or tragic things to happen, but He can absolutely make good come out of it if you are open to receive. Nothing is too hard for God. He knows the end from the beginning, and whatever your situation, it did not come as a surprise to Him.

Nothing surprises God. He is so awesome, so steadfast, so unshakeable. When you get out of the way and let God be God, there are no limits to what He can do. I serve an absolutely awesome God, as you will soon see, because He delivered me from much.

Even so, I needed His help daily. He did impress on me to be sure to tell Clint I had no desire to drive a big rig. I had a license to drive a car and a motorcycle, and that was enough. Besides, not being mechanically inclined, I definitely had no interest in driving a truck. He accepted that truth.

But there arose a different problem that I had to help Clint with, much to my chagrin. It became apparent that Clint needed help letting go of his late wife. I really thought the Lord would have walked him through that, so I was upset with God over this situation. What I mean is that Clint never had closure concerning her death.

He needed to be able to totally release her and let go before moving forward with me, even though we were already married. Not fun for either of us, but God's grace was sufficient (*2 Corinthians 12:9*). Clint had called me by her name two times, but never again once he received prayer, understanding, and closure, which helped both of us. I was reminded of something I had prayed at one point prior to meeting Clint.

I had prayed, *"Lord, don't you have someone that needs me?"* Hmmmmm. Maybe God looked at it differently since He knew what He had helped me through. I knew about the loneliness and pain of loss: my daughter had married, leaving me with a real case of empty nest syndrome; the next day my grandmother died; four months later my mother died suddenly; and five months after that my grandfather died, ending two generations. I certainly knew what it was to lean on God to cope effectively with painful issues of loss, so I could be a help to Clint.

It is good when mates have opposite strengths. I was aware of where God had made me strong, and now it was my turn to help my husband. Nothing we go through is ever in vain when we stay focused on the Lord. Sometime, somehow, somewhere He uses that experience further on down the road as only He can do. I guess that is why HE ... is GOD!

Six months after we married God called us to buy property in Texas. We decided to purchase land and a mobile home. I thought it was strange that my husband would not even look at a house near the edge of town, but I did not press the issue. So, our five acres about five miles from town became home. It was quiet in the country. The land was very flat and it was very peaceful, but that did not mean it was peaceful in our home. It was much to the contrary. I quickly discovered that Clint had a lot of anger in him, and that anger flared anytime and anywhere.

One time when we were in the truck on the interstate we had words. Clint got very angry and I suddenly felt him grab my long hair and pull my head backwards and towards him. I was in the jump seat. He held on, and as we continued to travel down the highway my back was pressed hard into the truck's gearshift.

He was yelling and would not let go. My back hurt! I could feel the gearshift pressing deeply into my back; it would shake as the wheels turned, causing me more pain. **Clint would not release me. At the same time, I prayed in my heart that God would not let us get killed. It was terrifying!**

Finally he let go. I landed back-first on the floor as he continued to yell. I managed to get myself onto the bunk, shaking and trembling in shock and pain but unable to cry. He finally stopped the truck. I told him the pain was so bad I needed help. He asked if I wanted to go to the hospital, and I heard myself answer with a feeble, "No."

He resumed driving, displaying no remorse, making no apology. In fact, he blamed me for nearly causing an accident! He had a way of turning things around to make it look as if I were at fault.

I know, I can hear you saying, *"Why didn't you go to the hospital?"* I toyed with the idea, but I knew they would fill out a report and that I would have to tell them what happened. We were in California at the time but lived in Texas. If the police took him away I would be alone and abandoned. I was afraid of that.

Also, I really couldn't think straight, the fear was so bad. In fact, as he continued to drive, I decided I had had enough. I would not live like this; death would be better. So I opened his pill container and looked for something that would put me to sleep for good. Wrong thinking indeed, but I have to tell you how I reacted to the abuse.

Before all this abuse happened to me I had never even spoken to anyone who had been in an abusive situation, or if I did I was not aware of it. I did not know what my options were—where could I go for help? What would happen if I did call the law? Rather than educating myself, I went into denial. It was easier to tell myself I must have provoked him and that it would not happen again. He was really tired, so I used that as an excuse.

But at the same time I knew he had stepped over the line in treating me that way. Furthermore, I felt like God had abandoned me, and that hurt much more than what my husband had done to me. God was in fact there all the time, but I was confused.

I had always seen God as my protector, my best friend, my Savior, and I had fully believed He would never allow such a thing to happen to me. Yet it did, so I was confused. My faith in God's ability to protect me was badly shaken after that incident. Fear caused me to withdraw from God a bit because my security was rocked. **Truth is, it was because of God that we weren't killed that night.** I know people were interceding. Thank God for intercessors!

While intercessors prayed, the battle was raging in my mind in the cab of that truck. I needed to listen to the Holy Spirit's voice within and be led by Him. My flesh—my carnal nature—was getting me into trouble because I was focusing on the circumstances. Faith sees beyond circumstances, knowing that circumstances are subject to change. My faith was severely damaged at that point.

I am a spirit, I live in a body, I have a soul (which is my mind, will, emotions) and I purposed to be led by the Holy Spirit. I knew He was my Master Mentor, Comforter, Teacher, Guide, and my Peace. For me to be led by the carnal nature or the soulish realm was leading me into trouble.

Being led by emotions or feelings will mess a person up, because emotions can change so easily and react to circumstances. Circumstances of fear, pain, fatigue, heartbreak, disappointment and discouragement affected my spirit man. I was beat up on the inside … far more than on the outside. Far more.

God never changes; He is always faithful. But my faith, developed over a decade at that time, was being shaken to the core. I was very broken; a broken vessel … who simply wanted a marriage that brought glory to God. Domestic abuse is not of God. The Bible says in *Malachi 2:16, Amplified* *"For the Lord, the God of Israel, says: I hate divorce and marital separation and him who covers his garment [his wife] with violence. Therefore keep a watch upon your spirit [that it may be controlled by My Spirit], that you deal not treacherously and faithlessly [with your marriage mate]."*

As I lay on that bunk in the truck, going down the road, I knew suicide would be very wrong. Besides, I also knew this would be my last trip on the road. THAT was one thing I did decide! Once I got home I would stay there. No more truckin' for me! Those days were done. I did not know what I would do, but I did know God told me right after the abuse in California that I was not to ever go on the truck again, for my own protection. This was my last truck run.

Part of me was relieved, yet part of me felt robbed because I really enjoyed being a partner with my husband on the road. I prepared meals and cleaned for him; I was "an extra set of eyes" helping him back the truck up, checking the side mirrors and reading the map. I also ministered to him by keeping him awake in the wee, small hours; keeping him company and encouraging him as he fought off depression, praying for him constantly.

I also enjoyed my ministry to the other truckers and their families. To see that door close was very painful, because when you are using your God-given gifts you are happy doing so. With a broken, bleeding heart I wrote a new song on the way back home to Texas.

## THE END OF THE ROAD

The clock's winding down
It's the end of the road for me
Time to pack up my gear
And call it history

My life will never be the same
This I know
Here's my truck key
No more can I go

I'll miss the moon and stars at night
And the view
All the bright lights
The dotted line too

My heart is squeezing forth
The tears with each mile
'Cause the big road
Has stolen my smile

Thank God for all the memories
Every one, and protection
God said
*"Your work's done."*

This is a brand new beginning for me
God is calling
His will I now see
So many souls are going to hell
This I know
I must help them
'Cause God loves them so

So what did I do with the pills? I took only one capsule of Clint's prescription medicine. I had such terrifying nightmares; I nearly went off the deep end, mentally!

When the effects wore off I repented and have never taken medications like that since. I learned my lesson. God saw my heart. He was there with me and helped me. Even though I felt He had abandoned me, in my heart I knew He was with me and would somehow help me. I knew without a doubt that He told me to stay off the truck, and that was just fine with me. I could hardly wait to get back home to Texas.

Despite the bad, good things had also happened out there on the big road, so I grieved because it was like losing friends. As the memories surfaced, both good and bad, I knew it was a part of my life that was fixin' to become history. Those days of truckin' were done for me.

I had mixed emotions because I was relieved as well as saddened. After all, you don't get much sleep out there on the road, and there is a lot of danger. It is somewhat like being a police officer—you have to be alert and on guard at all times. You learn not to turn your back. I recall us shutting down at a rest area in the wee hours of the morning. I was sitting in the jump seat and Clint was sitting on the bunk doing paperwork. Suddenly a man jumped on the running board of the driver's side and was looking at me face to face.

I froze; I was so scared because I did not know if he had a gun or not. I did not know if I was about to get my head blown off by someone who was drunk or who wanted drugs or was high on drugs already. I figured he had to be impaired or he would have known that he was risking his life because a driver might just blow his head off in defense! Kind of like how people just know not to touch someone's motorcycle, at least not without thinking twice about the possible repercussions!

My husband saw my mouth drop open in fear. He lunged forward with one sudden movement and the guy jumped down. He did not want to hang around, and I was certainly glad, but I did NOT want to park at rest areas any more, regardless of the hour.

So much for the trucking experiences. I just ask that you pray for the drivers that are out there and for their families because their calling, while so necessary, is not easy.

So I went home and used my writing talent, but first I got a lot of sleep in a comfortable bed and thoroughly enjoyed my own clean bathroom with all the extras. At least being home would have some perks.

As we arrived home, I removed all my things that had made the bunk "home" and cried as I moved out. My heart was severing its ties with trucking. It was very painful. It was like uprooting a plant that is too big for the pot and separating it into two plants. In doing so, all the roots have to be untangled, severed from each other, torn. Yet that pain was not as bad as being dead. God was protecting me. My emotions ran high.

I had been in all but three States in my short time of trucking. All in all, the windshield viewpoint was pretty awesome, and I was going to miss it.

# 6. AT HOME AT EASE

It didn't take long for me to learn that being at home would have its own set of difficulties. For one, the temperature was 100 degrees Fahrenheit every day for months on end. Our mobile home did not have central air conditioning. Central air was expensive; it would cost as much in our small mobile home as it would in a big house. But without it, I thought I would die from heat exhaustion.

We had something called a swamp cooler. It helped with humidity but this was dry air. After seven years of enduring intolerable heat, I pointed out to my husband that he was being unfair. He wouldn't even think of driving his truck if the air conditioning wasn't working, but he expected me to live without it. He got the point and realized that he was being selfish. So, we finally had it installed, and what a wonderful investment!

Being at home allowed me to get some greatly needed rest, get built up more with the Word of God, and look at the experiences on the road from a different viewpoint. God revealed a lot to me, but that did not mean I was ready to come out of denial and do something about it. Kind of like when you know the grass needs to be mowed but you put it off because you're tired. You don't feel like putting out the energy. Thankfully, God understood I was only human and not perfect. He did not condemn me; He kept loving me and drawing me closer and helping me to grow spiritually.

So how did my life change by being home? I got more sleep, spent more time in the Word and in prayer, and went to church and Bible study regularly. Yet, my heart was broken and needed to be healed, and God knew.

During one of my Bible studies, the teacher had a word of knowledge. He said there was someone who experienced something terrible, something that should never have happened. He said it was abusive and life threatening, and God wanted to minister healing to that person. I sat there and tears filled my eyes as I recalled the incident of the gearshift in my back. The teacher scanned the room until his eyes met mine. I was sitting in the third row and raised my hand just a little to acknowledge that I was the victim.

He nodded and simply said he would minister to me after the service was done. Tears ran down my cheeks. I realized God had been there during that horrible scene, and He cared for me enough that He showed someone else what had happened, and He wanted to help me. It moved me to more tears. That is love. Love never fails (*1 Corinthians 13:8, NKJV*).

After the service, I waited until nearly everyone was gone, except for several intercessors. They sat in their seats and continued to pray while the minister approached me. I saw the love and compassion in his eyes and it touched my heart deeply, but my mouth just would not open to tell him exactly what had happened. I was bound by shame.

He asked me if it was still continuing, and I told him it was not. He prayed for me, and I cried and cried as God healed and loved me back to life. A portion of me had died when that incident happened, and God knew it. He also cared enough for me to help me release all the pain of that memory and replace it with forgiveness and healing. I felt so much better when I left the church that day. It was a Divine appointment.

I had questions in my heart about why God let it happen. I knew God loved me, yet I also knew the devil could not do anything to me without first getting God's permission. Consequently, I was not coming to God with a completely open heart.

I felt like He had one arm open toward me with love, but that the other arm had a clenched fist. It wasn't true, but that is where I was at the time. That kind of thinking does not line up with the Word of God. If I had applied myself more to the Word and to prayer, God would have been able to set me free of that deceptive thinking.

The devil wanted me to believe God had let me down so I would trust Him less. The devil is the father of lies (*John 8:44*) and that was one of them.

God has never let me down. Circumstances may have LOOKED like it, but it was not true. Circumstances looked like Jesus lost when He died on the cross, but His death was necessary for the resurrection that led to our freedom!

But God was ministering to me. He always did. One time when I was still going out on the road, we got home from a three-week haul. I was so exhausted I decided not to go on the next trip. Within a few days I attended a prayer meeting at the church. Several people were in the sanctuary praying softly. They had made themselves available to pray for anyone that came in requesting prayer that day. I arrived, and when I got halfway across the sanctuary I could hardly walk, the burden became so heavy.

The Spirit of the Lord was all over me, and next thing I knew I was surrounded by people who began to pray. I did not tell them anything. I just received the prayer. Tears started to flow, streaming off my chin nonstop. I couldn't figure out where the tears came from, but they just kept coming.

The intercessors took turns leading in prayer while others prayed in the Spirit, using their heavenly language. I sat down because I was so weak, and God continued to minister healing to me.

I felt the pressure inside leave more and more. I was like a pressure cooker and someone had released the valve. You see, God will not allow more than we can bear (1 Corinthians 10:13). I was seeking Him for help, so He sent me to these faithful intercessors. I do not believe I would be alive today if it were not for their prayers.

It was amazing to me that I did not have to say a word about the reason for the extraordinarily heavy burden I was feeling. God knew, and the prayers continued until I could stand and smile again.

Spiritual surgery hurts, but it was much less painful than what would have happened if I had not received that much needed release. It was like a wound that had become infected and, if left untreated, was going to become gangrenous, spiritually speaking.

God had opened the door and prepared the way for my healing that day. He provided the people, and all I had to do was answer His call to *"Come"* (*Revelation 22:17*). He is no respecter of persons (*Acts 10:34*). He does not love me more than He loves you. When was the last time you answered God's call to *"Come"*? Don't wait until you FEEL like it. Respond to Him now.

It was because of my time talking with the Lord that I learned what not to do when my husband returned home after being on the road for a few weeks at a time. I had learned fairly quickly that when he came home I should leave him alone until he had at least one night's sleep. I would make him a meal, even if he came home at 4 a.m., but I would stay clear until he had slept. That was lesson number one.

I recall that when we would have words, he would get angry and would kick a piece of furniture or an antique. That would upset me because I treasured the antiques that had belonged to my late mother, and he treated them like they were junk. One thing would lead to another, and I soon realized he was jealous of my having things that meant a lot to me.

It seemed he was threatened by anything that gave me pleasure. I did not idolize the furniture, but I appreciated the beauty of the antiques. He began insisting we sell the pieces one by one because he did not like antiques. I finally gave in until all but one piece was gone; it was easier than arguing about it. However, I learned that doing what he wanted did not result in peace in our home. He controlled and got his way, but there was still no peace.

One day he smashed the large picture frames I had placed on one wall in the living room. I had purposely placed the photos of his two children, and those of his grandchildren, underneath his photo. Under my photo on the other side were photos of my two children as well as my grandchildren. It made a statement: family.

For some reason that I did not understand it upset him, and each time he looked at the photos he became angry until one day he broke some of the frames and glass. He showed no remorse and did not clean it up. I knew his behavior was wrong, but I did not know how to deal with him.

He was a grown man acting like a jealous, spoiled brat. It was obvious there was a lot of hurt and pain inside of him, yet I could not force it out. He had to deal with his own issues.

Why? Why the anger? Why such a severe reaction? I soon realized that when he got angry at me he resented our marriage and wanted his late wife to be alive. He wanted to mentally replace me with her but could not do it.

He also compared me with her, and this was damaging. God put me on the scene because I was the woman he needed then, but he could not accept that truth. The minute something happened that he did not agree with he would attack with words, anger, rage and destruction.

I insisted we both get some counseling and, to my surprise, he agreed. We went several times to a good church to get help. However, both parties must be willing to be completely honest; if not, it is like playing games with God.

During one of our sessions, the counselor told Clint his priorities were out of order and that he needed to spend more time at home. Clint's response was that he couldn't because trucking was the only job he knew. He honestly felt he could not do anything else and refused to look into possible options. So there was no change, no accountability.

The only change he ever made was changing jobs! When he got angry at his current boss, he would quit and go to another job until he got angry there too. He changed jobs at least ten times in the first several years of our marriage. When an issue arose, he would flee. That was his coping mechanism.

Our marriage counselor told Clint that if he broke something he must replace it immediately; he must show some responsibility. He didn't. In another incident he got angry when a friend gave me something that was dear to my heart. It was a silver tea set that was a special gift to me, replacing one from many years earlier.

Clint was extremely jealous that someone did something for me that meant so much to me. He picked up the tray and deliberately dumped the set on the floor, breaking two of the handles. It was $25 to solder each of them back on, and he refused to get it done. Jealousy consumed him. I could see it but did not know how to help him.

After that, he picked up a beautiful antique glass bowl and dropped it, smashing it to pieces on the kitchen floor. Part of me died with that bowl as I witnessed his obvious glee. The bowl was never replaced.

I quit going for counseling because Clint would not take the advice. Two different counselors told me, *"You have been hurt so deeply. I don't see how you stayed with him this long."*

My response was that my vows were made before God and divorce was not an option; I was committed for better or worse, and I had to believe that God would help us. Then when I got home I was upset because I went to a Christian counselor to get help and the counselor was talking about divorce. He gave up, but I didn't. I knew a divorce would not bring glory to God so that was not an option, but I knew we needed help. It was amazing the things Christians told each of us.

At one church I sat in the head counselor's office and briefly told him about the abuse, desperate for help. He said, **"You know, we are not equipped to handle abuse here."** I got really upset then and told him that he better get equipped because just that weekend a lady from the same church had called me with an emergency.

Her husband had thrown her against the wall, hurting her back, and she stayed with me for the weekend until she could find a place to stay until he got some help. I assured the counselor that in a congregation of several thousand people, this woman and I were not the only victims of abuse. It was like hitting a dead end when he said that to me. If the church couldn't help me, who could?

Some counselors would question why we stayed together. Some people would not want anything to do with us because they knew we had marital problems. We seldom got invited to anyone's home for fellowship. I had no social life since we had married, and that hurt because I loved people. I used to have lots of friends and enjoyed spending time with them, but now I found myself isolated and lonely. Abusers isolate their victims. The isolation should have been a red flag to me, but it wasn't. And although Clint had lived in same town most of his life, he didn't have any friends. That should have raised a red flag too.

I really did not mind being alone because I would busy myself writing books or songs or poetry, but dealing with loneliness was something that was new to me. Before this second marriage I had been walking with Jesus for thirteen years and I did not know what it was to be lonely. Jesus and I conversed daily; I knew Jesus as my spiritual husband (*Isaiah 54:5 says, "For thy Maker is thine husband: the LORD of hosts is his Name"* ) and best friend so I was never lonely. Actually it is the Holy Spirit I talk with, because Jesus sent Him after Jesus ascended to Heaven.

When it was just Jesus and me for the thirteen years that I was a single parent, I was never lonely. Then I had a husband to be my confidante, and I was lonely. It was bizarre. I never dreamt such a thing would happen. It was very painful.

I found myself wondering why God gave me a husband if I was just going to be at home for weeks at a time, by myself, while Clint was out of state. How could I be useful to God sitting at home day after day with nothing purposeful to do? I knew I could study the Word, but I was called by God to do more, to use what I learned from the Word.

There were people who were dying spiritually and I wanted to minister life to them. The few times I did go to the mall I could hardly stand to see the spirit of death in the eyes of so many people. It tore my heart. I wanted those people saved from their sin and from an eternity in hell. God had given me sharp discernment in that regard with other people, but when it came to my husband I was at a loss as to how to help him and how to have a marriage that brought glory to God. That was all I wanted. It was hard to keep encouraging myself, but I tried.

I was definitely an intercessor, but that did not consume enough hours of my time. Since I wanted a new car I told my husband I would pay for it if he would sign for me, and I would get a job. He agreed. I found a job in the deli department of a truck stop/travel center a few miles from home, on the afternoon shift. Guess who I got to witness to about Jesus? Truckers! Did God have a plan or not? You bet He did.

Did I want to cook hamburgers, fries, eggs and bacon over a hot grill? Not really, but I had learned how to recognize the hand of God in my life, and that made it all worthwhile. He was there with me and gave me **'Divine Appointments.'** By that I mean that he led certain people to patronize the truck stop, and I got to share Jesus with them.

How? Through encouragement, discerning if they were in a hurry or wanted to visit a bit while their food was cooking. I served each customer as if he were Jesus Himself in the flesh standing at that counter placing His order. I did my job as unto Him, "*And whatsoever ye do, do it heartily as to the Lord and not unto men,*" (*Colossians 3:23*). God honored my obedience. He sent people who were kind, who appreciated my being real with them, and who appreciated me being a lady.

I enjoyed my work and my contact with people. It was wonderful to recognize God preparing the way by giving me the job and the words to speak to my customers. I saw people's faces change from frowns of frustration to smiles of relief and peace whenever I had the opportunity to share my testimony and tell them about the goodness of God.

For example, one day after a customer—a trucker—finished his meal he came back to my counter, leaned on his elbows, and with a very serious face he said, *"I don't know WHAT you put in that hamburger ..."* (at which point I braced myself for a complaint) *"but THAT was one H____ of a HAMBURGER!!"* He kept staring at me with a question in his eyes. So I told him what the "Difference" was.

I leaned down, looked right into his eyes and in a voice only for him, not for the other patrons, I said, *"I always pray over the food before I serve it."* Then I smiled. He kept staring like a deer in the headlights, not changing position. As we looked into each other's eyes, his suddenly filled with tears as God witnessed to him my words of truth.

It was a special moment of seeing the hand of God at work because of a little prayer. God was listening and He answered. *Jeremiah 33:3 says, "Call unto me and I will answer thee…"* God is the reason I was there for a season, so to speak.

My home life often made it difficult for me to keep my chin up at work, but I did my best. I told no one of the difficulties on the home front. I figured they couldn't help me anyway. **Abuse is something that is not an everyday topic that women discuss, and women can discuss just about anything!** I resigned myself to the fact that I had made my bed, as the old saying goes, and I would have to lie in it. That kind of thinking did not provide much hope.

Even though God promoted me from that job to several other jobs over a period of several years, my situation at home was very grim. The job was a welcome relief, a place where I could see a smiling face once in a while and where I could feel useful as I served others. It helped me to press on, but the joy in my heart was gradually diminishing.

Abuse is kind of like erosion; you do not see the damage done on a daily basis. You just open your eyes one day and realize that a big part of you is gone … snuffed out with fear and confusion and heaviness. Needless to say, it's a rude awakening!

# 7. A RUDE AWAKENING

I TOOK A GOOD HARD LOOK at my situation, and it wasn't pretty. There I was in the USA while my two children and four grandchildren were in Ontario, Canada. I thank God for computers, because my kids and I kept our chat rooms busy. The printer was pretty busy too as we regularly exchanged photos. It helped to bridge the distance a bit, although it tugged at my heartstrings whenever I looked at the photos. You cannot hug a photo, and I was very much in need of a hug.

But God is so good; He met my need in such a delightful way. Just as I was thinking about how lonely I was feeling and how much I needed a hug, there was a knock on my front door. I opened it to three young children. The youngest lived next door and was about five years old at the time. He reached out with one arm and said, *"Hi, I just came to give you a hug."* I was so surprised I almost fell over! I believe God inspired him to do that. God used a little child to meet my need, and I was not going to fail to recognize the hand of God in my life. He can use whomever He chooses to use.

It was around this time that I was starting to think the counselors were right and that a divorce was necessary. But before I get ahead of myself, let me explain what was happening at our house. Clint's loud outbursts had become commonplace in our home, and there seemed no way of stopping them. I would try to talk to him about the situation after he settled down, but to no avail. He would not discuss any of our issues. His way of dealing with anything was to flee. Just flee.

When I attempted to confront him with the chaos of our lives, he accused me of putting him under pressure and he would leave. He would not discuss the situation or pray with me in an attempt to resolve the problem. He figured if he did not talk, we would not have any disagreements or strife and the problem would be solved. It was so disheartening.

I haven't met a woman yet that wants her husband to stop communicating with her. **Communication is to marriage what blood is to life!** Consequently, our marriage was dying more and more as we communicated less and less.

All I could do was pray myself. I could not change Clint and I knew it, but I could pray, and pray I did. I found myself reaching out to the Lord, spending more time in His presence. He healed and comforted me, but my marriage was still a mess. I felt better, but what about the marriage?

Years of praying and still seeing my marriage in such a bad condition had hurt my faith. Sad to say, it resulted in my pulling back in my prayer life. I had known it might take some time for things to get better, but after so many years my zeal to see answers and changes had waned. I really needed to see something concrete happen, and it just was not happening. If anything, the situation was getting worse and the violence was increasing. **Abuse always escalates.**

You may be wondering why I did not call 911 if the violence was increasing. Well, I did call them. There was one occasion in particular when Clint's rage escalated so much that I had to hide his hand gun. Clint had shoved me and grabbed my arms tightly at the same time. He threatened to hurt me as I ran to the master bedroom and called 911.

The police came and Clint's tone changed completely. He was like another person. He walked slowly and calmly into the living room and admitted to threatening, grabbing, and shoving me. However, there were no marks on me and there were no broken bones, so they did not charge him. They cautioned him sternly and told him to leave the house for 24 hours. This made him really angry. He threw his wedding ring on the floor and told me he would not be back.

Clint had a great fear of being imprisoned. When he was a young man he had served time in solitary confinement in the Air Force because he had gone AWOL two years after joining up. So, he took off that night, and I was left safe for a time but upset and heartbroken.

Another time, after yet another outburst of anger, I ran outside to the car. Clint pushed me backwards and I lost my balance, falling near the left front wheel. He picked up a large boulder and lifted it high above his head. All I could think of was "Goliath." I was so frightened I could not even scream. I was frantically trying to back up as I lay on the ground, but my shoes were sliding on the small stones in the driveway. My knees were bleeding from the fall. Finally, I heard a scream. Much to my surprise, it was mine.

It surprised him too, because I saw him freeze. Taking advantage of that moment, I rose to my feet and ran. I made it to my car, and as I put the car in gear he came after me with the boulder raised high, threatening to drop it through the windshield. I was leaning full blast on the horn; but we lived on five acres, as did each of our neighbors, so no one could hear me. Perhaps that was why he insisted on a house in the country and not in town. Isolation is insulation.

No one came to my aid; no one called 911. I continued to drive out of the yard. As I looked back, I saw he had dropped the boulder. With shoulders hunched, he walked slowly back into the house.

I drove to a Wal-Mart parking lot and parked near the edge of the lot to avoid being in sight of the traffic. It was getting dark, so I made sure I parked near a light. **Then I cried and cried and prayed and died a little bit more. Apparently no one saw or heard me. If they did, they did not let me know.**

I felt like it had all happened in slow motion and was trying to grasp the reality of the situation. I had never felt so alone in my life, or so helpless, or so sure that no one on earth cared if anything happened to me. It was horrifying. My faith in the judicial system was also shattered because I felt that unless I was half dead or had broken bones, they would or could do nothing.

As I sat there sobbing, I reflected on my life at that point. I just could not believe my life was in such an absolute mess. I knew my husband needed help, but he would not get any. He said the Veteran's Hospital was fine. But all they could do was to give him medication. He needed what only God could give.

Clint had a lot of fear from abuse in his childhood that had not been dealt with effectively. His father had been killed in a vehicle accident when Clint was a young boy, and that was very traumatic for him and his family. Then his mother remarried and his new stepfather was an abusive alcoholic.

Generally speaking, people who have been abused and who do not get help and healing remain emotionally crippled. They cannot mature emotionally past the age they were at the time of the abuse, and the cycle continues. But this is not too hard a thing for God to heal, as long as the person is willing to cooperate with Him.

Pride can get in the way and become a stumbling block preventing the person from getting help; he or she will remain emotionally stunted and disabled. It is sad but true. Yet, all the time Jesus is right there reaching out to take the hurt away, heal the wounds, and restore. He paid the price so no one has to live with stunted or frozen emotions.

But Clint was one of those people who refused to get help. As for me, I felt like I was a victim who was trapped because I married him in sickness and in health, and his being sick was not grounds for divorce. I thought adultery was the only ground on which Christians could divorce. As a result of this deception, I lived like a prisoner of war, gradually losing all hope.

One of the things that complicated Clint's problems was his medication. He took antidepressants for depression, as well as other medication for chemical imbalance. One of the medications caused impotence, but without the medication he was more prone to violence. This was very frustrating and emasculating for him, and I was a victim in more ways than one.

One time his doctor changed his medication and put him on a stronger antidepressant in addition to other strong prescriptions. I witnessed his increased anger, emotional highs and lows, and continually escalating restlessness. I knew I would have to move out if it kept increasing. I became so frightened that I visited his counselor at the hospital and made sure they had a report of the violence that was occurring. I told them that if anything happened to me, they would be responsible because of what this medicine was doing. I pleaded with them to change his antidepressant because he was threatening suicide, continually wanting God to just take him home to heaven. But at the same time he was full of anger that continued to build.

Around this time I was watching a program on Christian television and I heard a Christian medical doctor talk about the success his patients who had chemical imbalances were having with a new antidepressant. Hearing that doctor that day had to be a Divine appointment. I spoke to Clint's doctor. He changed Clint's prescription, and once the new medication had time to do its work, Clint improved noticeably.

**Once again, I recognized the hand of God at work. Just when I was about to throw in the towel, up came another answer. It was a bright light at the end of the tunnel.**

# 8. DIVINE PROTECTION

THE WEATHER WAS WARM, AND CLINT had left for work. During this time, God had inspired me to fast. I was not sure why, but I knew there was a reason so I obeyed. I just ate lightly, but no hot food. Little did I know the Lord was protecting my life. Literally!

Fasting from food helps me to be more sensitive to the Holy Spirit. I hear the voice of the Lord more clearly, and this time I had a very strong feeling about not eating. The feeling was so strong it was almost alarming. The first couple of days I only snacked on crackers, then realized I had lost my appetite completely. By then I knew the Lord was telling me not to eat, so I didn't. I drank liquids but had no hot food at all throughout the fast.

The prompting to fast was very strong, and since I didn't feel any hunger at all it was not hard to do. I did not know why I was fasting. In the past I had always known the purpose for the fast. Consequently, I did not know what to pray for or about, so I prayed in my heavenly language (*Acts 2:4*). For sure God had my attention and I was obedient, so I tried not to figure things out. As *Proverbs 3:5-6* says, *"Trust in the Lord with all thine heart; and lean not unto thine own understanding. In all thy ways acknowledge him, and he shall direct thy paths."*

At some point during the fast I noticed a slight scent of gas in the house and wondered about it. I had not used a gas stove before moving to Texas and was still a bit leery of it. Nevertheless, I just opened a window and kind of forgot about it after that.

Other windows in the house were also open because of the hot weather. This was when we still did not have central air conditioning. A few more days went by and I would occasionally get a faint whiff of gas, but it was windy outside; as the strong breeze blew through the house it took the odor with it, so I did not realize how strong the gas odor really was.

One morning I got up, and the wind must have died down because I very definitely smelled gas. I phoned the gas company and kept the windows open. Two servicemen arrived to check things out. Both servicemen were in the kitchen with the stove pulled out, checking behind it. Just then Clint returned home from work for the first time that week. He walked in the door, and just then I heard one of the serviceman say, *"This place should have blown sky high!"*

Stunned, I backed up until my back was against the wall. I looked at Clint and remembered that the gas odor started after he left, but because God had inspired me to fast I had not used the stove at all for the entire week. I believed, without a doubt, Clint had tried to kill me. It was a defining moment. I could not speak. I felt like the wall was holding me up. **NOW...I knew why God had me fast for those seven days. He kept me alive... because I did not use the stove one time!**

Both servicemen stood there looking at each other, then at Clint. He said nothing, just froze at the front door as if waiting to see what to do next. Then the second serviceman checked the gas and said the same thing: *"This house should have blown sky high ... the gas was on full!"*

No one said anything. No one called 911. I do not know what the servicemen wrote in their report, but I know the truth was not hidden from God. Clint's eyes got big, but he did not say a word. Not one word. The servicemen repaired the gas leak and left.

I cannot adequately explain how I felt. We did not discuss this incident. If I had been the one coming home from work to find out the gas had been turned up that high, I would have wanted to investigate and find out who had done it and why. I would have called the police, asked questions, demanded fingerprints. I would have wanted to find out who was trying to kill us! Yet no one spoke further about it.

Clint's eyes told me everything. For years I had prayed for sharp discernment, and it was paying off. Even if I didn't like what I was seeing, I knew God had answered my prayers. I was still alive!

The truth went so deep in my spirit that I felt like I was nailed to the wall and couldn't move. Then I began to wonder how many times in the past week Clint had been driving and saw the police behind him. Was he waiting for them to pull him over? Was he looking on the computer in his truck for a message to call the terminal? Was he edgy, nervous, remorseful, gleeful? What was he and who was he? I did not know him at all anymore.

When the proof is right in front of you that someone has tried to murder you by blowing you and your home sky high, how would you feel? I think part of me felt dead already. Life was being squeezed out of me day by day in ugly ways, yet I was still there, still breathing, still walking. I felt like a robot with no heart, no identity, no future—nothing but shattered dreams. Again, something in me died even more, and I lost my identity, my purpose in life.

Why didn't I call 911? I don't know. Why didn't the servicemen call 911? That is something I would really like to know. Were they intimidated by the size of my husband? I suppose I'll never know.

God kept me alive, but I wondered, *"For how long?"* If this almost happened, what was next? I thought that slapping a woman's face was as low as a bully could get, but this proved me wrong.

After this incident there were times when I would lay in bed next to my husband and wonder if he was going to try to kill me that night. I wondered if he would try to smother me. I could not sleep well and was relieved when he was not at home. At least I could sleep then. He might be home three days and gone two weeks, and each time he left it would take me almost the whole time he was gone to feel "normal" again. The emotional and mental torment was dreadful.

I searched my heart as to why he would want to do such a thing. What had I ever done that would make him hate me so much that he wanted to kill me? I did not have an answer, but I knew that God would not let that happen to me. I was naïve to the fact that I was blaming myself for his hatred. That is victim mentality, and I was a victim of domestic abuse.

Clint was a man who was easily offended and who would not forgive. Wrong doors are opened spiritually when someone who is easily offended refuses to forgive. Offenses build, anger deepens, and the poison of that leads to bitterness and can eventually lead to murder if not dealt with appropriately. Many people have died for these very reasons. *"The thief cometh not, but for to steal, and to kill, and to destroy: I am come that they might have life; and that they might have it more abundantly,"* (John 10:10).

My trust was in God, and He would not let me down. He taught me to proclaim the Word and I did. *Isaiah 54:17 says, "No weapon that is formed against thee shall prosper; and every tongue that shall rise against thee in judgment thou shalt condemn. This is the heritage of the servants of the LORD, and their righteousness is of me, saith the LORD."* Praise God. I typed out these scriptures and proclaimed them daily. The only thing I had was the Word of God. Either it worked or it didn't. I believed it did. I was still alive! Praise God.

But now I had to decide what to do—stay in the United States with Clint and try to make the marriage work, stay in the United States by myself, or move back to Canada. It wasn't an easy decision for me. I was concerned that if I returned home to Canada, separated from Clint but not divorced, I might be responsible for half of any debt he might incur. That move did not appeal to me. I also felt challenged to try to make my marriage work. I thought if I left I'd be a "quitter," and I was determined to have a marriage that brought glory to God.

Before I go any further it is important for you to know that although I was a Spirit-filled Christian serving the Lord for over twenty years, I was deceived and in denial.

I was deceived by thinking it was wrong to divorce a man who abused me and who, I believed, even tried to kill me. My love for the Lord and my desire to be obedient were so strong that I flat out would not consider divorce; I thought the only way a Christian could get a divorce was on the grounds of adultery. This deceptive thinking put me in great danger, but I didn't see it at the time.

People in the world (non-believers) often go from one marriage to another thinking almost nothing of it; many bail out the minute the going gets rough, and commitment is a word that is foreign to many of them. For me, though, I had vowed a covenant vow to my husband and to God, and I thought that I had to keep that vow at all costs. I believed that because there was no adultery (that I knew of), divorce was not an option. But I was wrong. I should have divorced him years before for the abuse.

God says in His Word, *"My people are destroyed for lack of knowledge,"* *(Hosea 4:6)*. I was being destroyed because of my lack of knowledge of the truth of God's Word. He was providing a way out with divorce, but I was keeping myself in danger and bondage by staying in the marriage, not realizing God would not condemn me for doing what I needed to do to be safe and to stay alive.

And I was in denial—denial of the danger I was in and of my ability to "fix" it. Even though I was convinced Clint had tried to kill me by turning the gas up; even though he told me he would lie awake in bed thinking of ways to kill me; **even though he once told me he would smash my face so much that no man would ever look at me again;** I somehow put all that aside and tried to go on with the marriage and make it work.

I think it was just much too painful to face the truth of such actions and statements. They made me wonder what kind of a woman I must be if he felt like that. Somehow, for him to have such thoughts, it seemed like it must be my fault.

When pain is too much to cope with, it is easier to go into denial. Denial will actually create a bigger problem in the long run, but it feels easier in the moment. It is a coping mechanism, but it can be a deadly one.

While I tried to decide what to do, I did seek counsel from pastors and their wives and other leaders at several different churches. But I always downplayed the degree of abuse I was experiencing and I never told a soul about Clint's threats against my life. Because I didn't give them the full story, only once did a pastor say something to the effect that I should divorce Clint for abusing me.

This pastor had helped his daughter get a divorce when she was the victim of domestic abuse, and he said he would never let her live like that. She had since remarried and was happy. Yet, he did not support it with scripture, so I figured he must be wrong and I did not want to be disobedient to God. So I stayed deceived, married, and with little hope of relief.

Clint was extremely jealous and insecure. In my efforts to help him feel better about himself I would compliment him and do all I could to encourage him. Encouragement is my gift from God, so it comes without any effort. Nevertheless, there came a time when I saw how I was being drained by pumping him up all the time, while he was perfectly content to bask in all the attention.

He made no effort to get up on his own two feet and start pressing on or start maturing in his relationship with the Lord. He was like a baby that always wanted a pacifier. He did not want to grow up and accept responsibility for anything. After a while I ceased being the encourager and expressed my disappointment with his lack of initiative. It felt like each time I leaned on him at all it was like leaning on a partially deflated balloon; the support was not there. I had to transfer my leaning to the Lord.

In fact, everyone needs to know how to lean on the Lord Jesus Christ, because sooner or later people will let us down. Jesus will never let us down. He is there all the time. I learned that when He sent the Holy Spirit to teach me and to be my Comforter and Best Friend, He provided exactly what I needed regardless of my marital status. *John 14:26 says, "But the Comforter, which is the Holy Ghost, whom the Father will send in my name, he shall teach you all things, and bring all things to your remembrance, whatsoever I have said unto you."*

As you read this book, I pray that you will come to know how much Jesus loves you and that you can trust Him to help you too. He is the Best Friend you will ever have, and as your Savior He will fill a void only He can fill. Only Jesus saves … that is profound truth.

God had protected me from a gas explosion, but I now needed to be protected from Clint's self-pity and total self-centeredness. If I was not careful I would be worn out pumping him up continually with words of encouragement.

Christians who do not mature do not bring glory to God. We cannot stay baby Christians forever and be in God's perfect will. Just as a child is expected to grow, so it is with God's children. Getting saved is just the first step. Growing is a result of becoming a disciple of Christ, and it is progressive.

I learned it is kind of like an intimate conversation—it has to be two-way. One person cannot do all the communicating while the other person simply keeps receiving, or the giver will give out! God requires balance in all things, and Jesus is our example. I knew that if I continued to keep pumping Clint up I would burn out, because God was showing me to hold back and give him time to apply himself.

# 9. BULLY/MASTER BULLY

AFTER CLINT AND I HAD BEEN married a few years, he showed me a newspaper he had saved that had published an article about him. The article told what he was like before becoming a Christian and the changes afterward. The article was entitled "**Bully**". It surprised me because that did not sound like a very edifying title for an article in a Christian paper meant to glorify God.

Nevertheless I read it, but I found myself not wanting to think about it. The article told about a side of Clint that I had come to know, and I did not know how to deal with him when he acted like a bully. It revealed to me that this was not something that suddenly began when I came on the scene, so I certainly was not the cause.

Knowing I wasn't the cause felt like a shallow comfort, though. As long as I thought I was the cause, I took comfort (misguided though it was) in thinking I could do something to stop it. But I was beginning to see there was nothing I could do. Only God could heal Clint, and even then only if he allowed God to work in him. In the meantime, the abuse continued.

Here is another incident that took place in our home, such as it was. You know, I've no doubt that most people like to think of their home as a safe haven. How sad when it isn't.

One day Clint was upset about something. He reached out and shoved me backwards. I lost my balance and fell to the floor. Fear had raised its ugly head again. I was down! I backed into the spare bedroom that we used for storage. Clint kept approaching me angrily. I was frantically scooting backwards, trying to get to the bed so I could pull myself back up again and regain my balance.

He waited until I stood up, then just as I stood he shoved me again and I fell backwards toward the bed. As I fell sideways my hip and arm hit some boxes of books that were stored there. I slid to the floor, pulling my shoulder as I landed crookedly. Instinctively I tried to get up, because my mind could not think of anything except escape. Such fear paralyzes. As I tried to get up, Clint pushed me again. I saw his eyes and knew he was getting great pleasure out of tormenting me. I thought to myself, "*He is so sick.*" He was thrilled with this sick, controlling power. **It did not cross my mind at the time that I was ENABLING this abusive behavior!!** Both of us needed help, needless to say.

I tried to get up while straddling the boxes on the floor. At the same time I was trying to back up a bit, but there was very little space because of the boxes stacked up in the room. Just as I was almost up on both feet he shoved me again and down I went. There was no place to sit because of the boxes, and I bumped into things as I fell. He was screaming at me all the while. I prayed, asking God for wisdom to diffuse the situation. I stayed on the floor, trying not to cry or move. Clint kept yelling at me. His big steel toe boots were so close to me he looked ten feet tall, like Goliath.

I stayed down and told him to leave or I would start screaming. I was no match for his size, and I knew it. He knew it too. It was so devastating and humiliating to see how he actually enjoyed tormenting me. I knew it was wrong and sick, yet I did not understand why a man would do such a thing.

Even though it happened years ago, it still makes me cry as I write about it because sometimes the seemingly simple abuse (if there is such a thing) really does result in damage. **It wounds a woman's spirit when she is violated, and I was violated.** It brought shame, hurt, rejection, loss of respect, and a feeling of helplessness, not to mention shattered dreams and trust. There is not one woman in the world who ever even thinks such things would happen when she stands at the altar on her wedding day. I had never once seen my parents engage in any behavior that was even remotely abusive, and I naively expected my marriage to be peaceful too. It was not.

When Clint turned and left the room without helping me up or saying he was sorry, I breathed a sigh of relief. But then I had another thought—maybe he was playing some kind of sick game, waiting until I got up, then he would return and begin again. In fear, I listened for his footsteps to fade, and then I got up. I honestly don't remember what happened after that. I know I shed tears from a broken heart, but beyond that I draw a blank.

No physical pain, but the emotional and mental hurt were palpable. I was walking around like a porcupine with the quills on the inside; each one there as a result of pain inflicted. Only God's love and forgiveness could remove the quills and heal.

As I sought the Lord for help, He spoke to me of my need to forgive; then He opened the wounds, healed them, filled them with His love, and sealed them shut. Now, as a result, I am stronger than ever before in those areas. I was learning how to get the victory more quickly.

As you read this book I realize it sounds so terrible that I went through all of this yet stayed with my husband. As I said earlier, I was deceived into thinking I had no choice. But God protected me and I learned a lot as I grew closer to the Lord. These incidents did not occur weekly by any means, though each incident never should have happened. Nevertheless, over a period of eleven years of marriage to a bully, at times my life was a 'silent hell.' I was wrong to enable Clint, yet in my mind divorce was not an option. So I had to try to put my situation in perspective as a way of trying to understand it.

This is not the best illustration, but it comes to mind so here goes. If you had a dog that bit someone once, but not again for the next three years, you would tend to let your defenses down and become more trusting of that dog. Is it not the same with human beings?

I also thought that while divorce would protect me, it would not help him or protect other women from him. On the other hand, I realized that even if I were able to help Clint, it would not stop him from fooling around with another woman and hurting her too.

I kept praying, reading and searching for answers, all the while saying little to friends about what was happening. But people did know. One time we had company over for dinner. I forgot about my bruises and wore a short-sleeved top. My one arm was fully black and blue underneath. As I reached for the fridge door, I heard my guest gasp. I turned to see what was wrong and she had turned the other way, not saying a word. The shock silenced her. I had forgotten I was so bruised, so I did not realize until later why she had gasped.

Afterwards, I was glad—glad someone else knew, yet what good did it do? I am sure others had seen bruises on my arms from Clint's fingers, but too often people do not want to get involved so they turn away. It is easy to understand why people tend to shy away from a couple who has marital problems, yet that couple needs friends then more than ever. They need support.

What would Jesus do? Run away from, or run to, the hurting hearts? I am so thankful that He didn't run from me. He was there all the time and held me in His arms of compassion, wiped away my tears, comforted me and just let me know that He would not leave me. No person on this whole earth can comfort you like Jesus can. He goes right to the depth of your heart, and with His love He reaches in and refuses to let that hurt stay in there, festering and poisoning you.

When Jesus heals, He does a perfect job. He does not mess around; He finishes what He begins. There are no loose ends left because Jesus is always thorough and detailed, overlooking nothing. In fact, there was a purpose in everything Jesus did—a purpose for every step He took, each word He spoke, each time He reached out with those wonderful carpenter's healing hands, so calloused yet so tender. It was Jesus who gave me a reason to press on, to not give up. He gives life and puts zeal and determination within as He is taking the hurt out. No wonder He is such a healing Jesus!

But what about incidents like these when there is pushing and shoving, but no actual slap or backhand or fist to the face—when there is physical abuse but no bruises or marks? Is that why it was so easy for me to cast it aside, trying not to think about it, hoping and praying things would get better, denying the seriousness of my situation and not recognizing that it was doing a great deal of damage? I learned it was easier and less painful to go into denial than it was to deal with the issues. **I also learned that abuse always, always escalates!**

There came a time when I kept a small piece of luggage packed in the trunk of my car. It was there for months, in case my husband flared up again and I had to leave for my own protection. I had the basic amenities at hand, but I must tell you that when I opened the trunk to put groceries inside and saw the luggage, it was like a red flag reminding me of all the previous incidents. Each time I saw that luggage it was like a jolt to my spirit, kind of like an unexpected shock jolting me awake, out of my stupor of denial. It prompted me to deal with my problems, not to ignore and endure them. Finally, one day I took it out and left it out. I decided that keeping the luggage there meant I was expecting trouble, but I was expecting things to get better. The only problem was that if you want things to get better you have to do something different.

There were times when I would sit down and try to figure out why a man would treat his wife so badly. Nothing I thought of would even come close to justifying such behavior. Why do this to someone you love? Obviously he was hurting and had not healed; he had not learned to manage anger and was ruled by his emotions so he could not walk in love. Why would such an unhappy person not want to get help unless he was deceived about something?

Or … unless he was getting something out of his behavior, such as a high from the power gained through controlling someone! His thinking was very different; he had established a pattern of obnoxious behavior that he had learned from his stepfather who regularly came home drunk and abused his mom. Yet Clint did not drink.

Nevertheless, he was raised in an environment where emotional out-bursts were commonplace. Could it be that he would subconsciously or even consciously cause such outbursts to erupt in an effort to meet a deep-rooted need? Sick? Yes, but true. Why could he not stand to have complete silence in the home, or even have a lull in the conversation if we had company? Why the need to keep talking just for the sake of saying something, anything, rather than listen to the silence? Fear. Fear of losing control.

He was afraid someone else would control the conversation and it just might result in a finger being pointed at him, so he controlled the conversation to the point that we no longer had friends visit, nor did we get invited anywhere. We had no social life at all. We did not go anywhere together except to church and the grocery store, and about three times a year we went out to dinner together.

Violence was commonplace throughout Clint's childhood. He was abused by some of the people he was sent to live with when his mother was ill. Between those memories, as well as those of his mother being beaten regularly by his alcoholic step-father, the affect was profound.

For example, Clint told me about a doll carriage and other toys that were smashed under the Christmas tree when his stepfather fell into them in a drunken stupor. It affected Clint so much that he did not even want a Christmas tree, even though the incidents had happened decades earlier. He hated Christmas and called it nothing but commercialism.

When we did go to church I found it very difficult to stay focused on the Lord because it was one of the few times that I had my husband beside me. Once in a while he put one arm around me or held my hand in church. I reveled in the physical attention, because it was a need that was not otherwise being met. So we appeared to be close when in church, but it was a mask, just a momentary fleeting contact. When we returned to the car his mouth soon gave way to things his carnal nature wanted to say, and next thing I knew it was so bad I wanted to leave him in the car and walk home.

In fact, once when I was driving I returned to the church and left him in the car parking lot while I went inside and told one of the pastors I could not take any more. Clint's yelling and shouting when I was driving was endangering us on the road. He just wouldn't stop ranting and raving, so I stopped the car and told him to get out or to stop yelling. He did, but only after I started the car again. It was a tormenting spirit manifesting.

I knew better than to cast a spirit out of someone who does not want to be free or to continue in the ways of the Lord. I also knew it was not Clint I was fighting. The battle was a spiritual one, against the demonic forces he was yielding to. Knowing this was one of the main reasons I did not leave him.

I believed he needed me and he needed to get victory, and I wanted to see that happen for him. Yet I could not make it happen no matter how much I prayed. You see, his free will was involved. God looks at the heart. Nothing is hid from Him. *Ephesians 6:12 NKJV* says, *"For we do not wrestle against flesh and blood, but against principalities, against powers, against the rulers of the darkness of this age, against spiritual hosts of wickedness in the heavenly places."*

The pastor went out and talked to Clint in the parking lot, but Clint would not get out of the car, nor would he apologize to me. He continued the behavior until it got so bad that I told him if he would not behave in the car he would have to take his own car and I would drive mine. He didn't like to drive when he was home since he drove an 18-wheeler all week. But, I meant what I said, so for months we drove to church in separate cars.

I sat in church knowing it looked like **"all was well."** But I was so glad that God knew everything. It helped me so much knowing that He did not miss a thing, that He was fully aware of every incident. He knew the times I said things that I shouldn't have, times I repented to Him and to my husband, and times that I tried desperately to diffuse the situation.

God knew it all, and it is our Heavenly Father who knows how much we can bear. Sometimes we do not realize how much pressure we are under until we are ready to snap, but God knows, and when we are yielding our spirit to Him, He will clearly direct our path. He did this for me, and that is why I am now writing this book.

God knows how many times you try to make things better; how many times you pray; how many times you pour out your heart to Him; how many times you praise Him with a sacrifice of praise; how many times you feel like giving up; how many times you stay awake at night in fear; how many times you turn it loose and tell Him you would serve Him anyway, regardless of how tough life's circumstances become because you know He is right there with you.

But, He does not want you to be abused by anyone, whether you are a man or a woman. He wants you to take spiritual authority over that situation. It is the devil that comes to steal, kill, and destroy. Jesus came to give us life and that more abundantly (*John 10:10*). So you rebuke Satan in Jesus' Name, having first submitted yourself to God, and Satan will flee. Then what? Praise God for the victory. At least that is what I thought. So I did what I knew to do. I submitted myself to God, covered myself with the blood of Jesus, put on my armor, and tried to walk in love. But I still got hurt and I didn't understand, so I began to question God. It hurt my faith severely.

Why? Because it looked like my husband could treat me however he wanted to and get away with it. I prayed and prayed and bound and loosed spirits and praised God. Yet things escalated further and further. It was like quicksand and I knew it, but I couldn't seem to get out.

Remember, there was a lot of denial on my part so I had blocked out many of the previous incidents. The mountain seemed like a little hill as far as my memory bank was concerned. It had become a habit to deny the memory of those painful incidents ... it was my coping mechanism. However, there is a big difference between coping and having victory, victory in Jesus

I am trying to let the words be pulled up from the depths of my heart, and to be completely transparent with you because I want you to get free too. If I am completely honest with you, I will tell you it is absolutely incredible for me to read these pages and realize I suffered so much yet did nothing about it. My first impulse was to kick myself again and again and again, to no avail. Then there was embarrassment, because I was embarrassed to tears to realize I put up with so much abuse and did not know why. I had become an enabler! It was horrifying.

How could I have been so stupid, so deceived, so blinded, such a fool? But then, I knew condemning myself was not going to help me at all so I put a stop to that. Yet you need to know that was my first reaction when God revealed the denial I was in and set me free. It hurt—it hurt a lot, but it hurts to remove slivers. Yet it is necessary or the result would be even more damaging. So what does that tell you? It tells you **there is pain in getting healed, but there is greater and more long-lasting pain in denial, so why not choose healing?** Jesus paid the price for everyone to be healed.

I wish I had done something about the abuse then because abuse escalates, as you will see in the next chapter. Sad to say, the abuse did get worse, but read on because God has a purpose in your doing so. He isn't asking me to become like a glass house, totally transparent, so people can point a finger at me or judge me. He wants to use this book as a tool to help others who are in denial and in abusive situations. Trust me, God has a purpose, so keep reading and I will keep writing. Which do you think is easier to do?

# 10. PREMEDITATED BLATANT BACKHAND

It was a quiet afternoon, but it sure did not stay that way for long. Clint was getting ready to leave for work, and he said something to me to which I responded, *"You shouldn't say that."* *"Why not?"* he asked. I answered, *"Because you shouldn't talk to me like that. As a matter of fact, I should kick your butt for talking to me like that."* *"Go ahead,"* he said. I looked up at him.

He had his back turned to me. I thought about what it would be like to give him a kick in his backside and almost giggled, but decided against it. Then he repeated, *"Go ahead."* I did giggle then because it sounded so funny since he is such a big guy. As I looked at his backside I just lifted one foot a bit and attempted to kick his butt jokingly. My foot hit the floor, and in a split second the world exploded like a grenade in my face.

Out of the corner of my eye I saw something dark rushing toward my face, and before I could see what it was I was hit. Clint backhanded me square on the right side of my face and chin. He was holding a leather shaving kit when he hit me, and the force of it knocked me right off my feet. I fell backwards into the writing desk … knocked everything off it and hurt my arm and side as I fell to the floor.

Clint just stood there, looking at me. I could see the smugness in his face. He felt good about his power over me. He looked like someone who had just landed a solid blow of defeat to his enemy.

I was shocked that he had actually struck me. The pain was so bad that I could hardly move. My jaw hurt so badly that for the next week, every time I opened my mouth to eat it hurt because it was out of alignment. My head felt like I got hit with a sledgehammer. Not that I would know what a sledgehammer feels like, but you can use your imagination.

It was a severe blow to the head from a 250 pound, over six-foot bully. Not a man. A real man does not strike a woman. My heart was asking,

"*Why?*" We weren't even arguing, we were joking about the kick in the butt. Correction, I was joking. He had a plan. Then I realized what had just happened. He set me up. He planned to do that … in fact he asked me twice to kick him. And I took the bait. I felt so helpless and defeated. Manipulation is cruel.

I felt such fear and disappointment. I mistakenly believed that if I called 911 they would charge me with assault since I kicked him first. Even though he had asked me to, I was sure he would deny it. **I was so much in pain, yet my heart hurt worse than my face and jaw! Far worse!!!**

Despite the pain, nothing was broken except the leather shaving kit. It was nearly a foot long and about six inches wide. When Clint hit me with the case, he struck so hard that his right thumb pierced through the leather and poked a hole in the case which was zippered shut. The hole was not near a seam either. It was caused by brute force.

What did he do then? I wondered what he would do. Was death next? He watched me move like a bird with a broken neck and looked to see if I was getting the phone. I walked towards the bedroom to lie down because inside I just wanted to die. It was horrible. At that point I didn't care if he followed me and finished me off or not. It probably would have been a relief. At least that was my thinking at the time. Never in my life had such a thing happened. I lay there and couldn't even cry because crying made my jaw hurt more.

He left for work, no apology. In fact, he said I shouldn't have kicked him. Abusers have a way of turning things around to make the other person feel they are to blame. Abusers take no responsibility, at least Clint didn't, nor did he show any remorse whatsoever. That was a huge red flag not to be ignored; but ignore it I did. **Ignorance is costly.**

**For a whole day I just lay in pain and shock.** Then I went to church and got an appointment with one of our pastors and his wife, and I told them what had happened. They prayed for me. But, they did not tell me to call the law. They did not tell me that a Christian does NOT have to live with an abuser. I should have separated from him for my protection because he broke covenant with me. Abuse is not love and protection.

They did not advise me to leave him. Nor did they know that I was wrong about the law charging me with abuse if I had called them. I had assumed that was what would happen because of bits and pieces of things I had seen on television. It is not good to assume things. Get the facts. Let the law decide. Call them. That is what they are there for.

Unfortunately both pastors failed to confront my husband at all. They did shun him, but according to scripture the first step is for a godly brother or sister (depending on the gender of the offender) to confront the offender and help him (or her) get back on track. Then, if the offender does not heed the truth, the church should send two people and try again. The next step, if the offender has not repented, is to take the matter to the leadership for them to confront the offender. Finally, if there is no change, no repentance, the person is excommunicated from the church (*Matthew 18:15-17*).

If church officials had spoken to him one on one in an effort to help him, fine. But that is not what happened. They shunned him ... with no explanation whatsoever! To me, that was unmerciful and caused more damage. Who knows what the result may have been if things had been handled scripturally.

Wisdom is needed in the church, and it is also needed in the world with regard to how the law works. I grabbed an opportunity to learn when the police came to the house in response to a 911 call. It was a few years after the fact, but I asked them if my husband would have been arrested for backhanding me. The officer looked me in the eye and said most emphatically, **"You SHOULD have called US!!"** Clint was there and heard the answer. He never hit me again. I believe that the words from an authority figure— the police officer—brought the fear of the Lord on Clint. "*The fear of the Lord is the beginning of wisdom: and the knowledge of the holy is understanding,*" (*Proverbs 9:10*), and as I said, he never hit me again.

It is so interesting to see how God works. Clint had called Information to get someone's phone number, and by mistake he dialed 911 instead. Even when you explain to them that it is not an emergency, they have to check it out. So the police came to the house, and that was when I asked them about whether or not I should have called them years earlier. Who but God knows what I was protected from, perhaps that very day.

The law is there to protect us. I took the law into my own hands when I made that foolish decision. Not wise. Pastors are still learning too, so discernment is needed when receiving counsel. I was influenced by how they handled the situation in simply shunning Clint without explaining why.

Obviously they did not realize I needed a restraining order for protection. Who knows, maybe that would have resulted in Clint's getting some help. I just know I learned the importance of praying daily for sharp discernment. I also realized that people will let me down eventually. God is the only One Who will never let me down, so my trust must be in Him.

The mind is the battleground. The devil can only defeat a Christian through deception. I was deceived into thinking I would be charged with assault. Consequently, I needed to have my mind renewed more with the Word of God. God, in His love and care for us instructs us (His children) to renew our minds with the Word. It is vital to our success to just do it. *Roman's 12:2 says, "And be not conformed to this world: but be ye transformed by the renewing of your mind, that ye may prove what is that good, and acceptable, and perfect, will of God."*

The more our mind is renewed by the Word of God—the Bible—the more prepared we are to be led by God. When we have to make a quick decision it will be done with godly wisdom and the Holy Spirit's leading, not with emotions riding high or religious thinking getting in the way. When the carnal nature leads we will not know victory. When we do things God's way He will prove Himself faithful every time.

This reminds me of yet another incident, but this time I was not the victim. I was teaching Sunday school with about eighteen students in the class. One little girl, about four years of age, arrived with a severely swollen and blackened eye. She was with her two sisters, and one of the sisters told me their daddy hit the little girl. I felt sick to my stomach. I prayed for her and it was a very solemn time. As soon as class was over I contacted the pastor and told him about the situation.

I figured he would call the police and there would at least be an investigation. Instead, his response set my spirit ablaze with indignation, and it has bothered me ever since. I was told they had to be careful about that kind of thing and about getting involved. He told me I did the right thing in telling him about it, but they had to be careful of possible retaliation. Since that time I have learned that whether the pastor reported it to the law or not, I should have. It is required by law that such a violation be reported.

To this day I do not know if that little girl ever got any help, because shortly after the family moved away. I submitted to the authority of the pastor and did not call the law, but I did not agree with that decision. I saw it as giving in to fear, and fear like that is not from God.

Our faith is in God to protect us from any retaliation, and our job is to do all we can to help the weak ones. **We must not let fear cause us to become compromising Christians.** I see that child's face many times and pray for her, but only God knows what else she might have been protected from had the father gotten the help he needed. I learned from the experience, but at too hefty a price.

At that time in my life I did a lot of thinking about leaving my husband. I was very much aware that the abuse was escalating and did not want to ever hurt more than I did at that point. He was away maybe two weeks at a time, sometimes less, but I always knew he was coming back and did not know what to expect upon his return.

I did not have the finances to go back to Canada or to get an apartment somewhere in town and pay for a move. Money is power, and when you just don't have it you are powerless to do much of anything (or so I thought). My options seemed pretty slim and pretty grim.

While he was away, Clint would continue to call me long distance and tell me he loved me. But love is an action word, and his actions towards me were not loving. I grieved a lot over the fact that our marriage did not bring glory to God. I felt trapped because I thought I could not divorce him and because he did not think change was necessary. I knew I could not change him, yet I could not be productive. We just kept pulling in opposite directions like a team of horses that were unequally yoked.

There were so many unresolved issues between us, and I prayed so many prayers, yet the nightmare continued. Clint's medication did not prevent him from having sex, but his way to control was to withhold sex from me. That is a form of manipulation, which is witchcraft. Spouses are not to withhold from each other sexually except during a time of mutually agreed upon prayer and fasting: *Defraud ye not one the other, except it be with consent for a time, that ye may give yourselves to fasting and prayer; and come together again, that satan tempt you not for your incontinency,* (1 Corinthians 7:5).

I spent most of my time searching my heart to get healed and was fearful of becoming bitter. I was determined not to let the enemy win. I knew it was a spiritual battle. Daily I spoke more scriptures over our marriage and stood on the Word of God. *"Can two walk together except they be agreed?"* (Amos 3:3) That is also the Word of God, and He will not violate anyone's free will.

My husband suffered severe depression. I am not giving any labels, because if the doctors knew what was really wrong they would have been able to help him. He had a death wish that tormented him regularly. God gave me discernment to know when this occurred. I prayed and bound that spirit, so while Clint didn't really want to live, he was prevented from committing suicide.

Being an intercessor is a high calling and not to be underestimated. More can be accomplished through prayer than through anything else. Darkness was held back for years and my spiritual muscles were developed through it all. My prayers were not in vain.

The hospital kept changing his medication and the amounts were increasing. I spoke with two of his psychiatrists, and it didn't take long to learn they really weren't going to tell me anything. He was the patient and I was the wife. The fact that they kept changing his medication told me they didn't know how to help him either. No matter what they did, it was only a temporary fix.

Clint suffered a lot because he trusted the doctors to know how to help him. His frustrations were great because he still had four mental break-downs in eleven years. He was off work with no income for months at a time. It made victims of both of us because we were both affected by his illness. I was trying to educate myself about his condition by speaking with the doctors, to little avail. I learned to draw what I needed from the Lord. I had to be strong for my husband.

I recall his mother saying that to me just after we first met. She said, *"I know you are the right woman for my son; you are strong. I see that strength in you and I know you are the right woman for him."* At the time I thought it strange that I had to be so strong and wondered what she meant. I soon found out.

# 11. A THIRD VOICE

Mental health problems were not the only problems we faced. I caught Clint lying to me about another woman who was employed at the same place as he was. I went to the truck terminal with him one night and she was on duty alone in the guard shack. We drove up in our pick-up vehicle and he walked in first. She blushed and her eyes filled with tears as they made eye contact. Then she saw me behind him. Words were not necessary. She knew I knew she was interested in him. I looked at my husband. He had tears in his eyes and his cheeks were flushed. It was a defining moment. I felt sick to my stomach. My heart sank. I got the picture, and a picture is worth a thousand words. I said nothing.

Soon he and I walked to the 18-wheeler to fuel up. He was going to leave his pickup truck at the truck yard, then he was going to drive me home in the 18-wheeler after he fuelled up and would then go on the road for several days. This little outing before he left was something we did occasionally, because it gave us a little more time together. This time, though, was not very pleasant. As he began fuelling the truck, the Lord spoke to me. (**God knows everything and He wanted me to know something. The Holy Spirit said,** *"Your husband feels sorry for her because she is out here in the yard doing her job throughout the night."*)

Did God tell me that to hurt me? No! Of course He didn't. He gave me the heads up for a purpose. He wanted me to speak up and expose the darkness because He revealed to me by His Spirit that they were spending too much time together talking. She was lonely and there was an attraction there. My job was to bring light to expose the darkness.

When we finished fuelling up and got in the truck I confronted the issue. In a nonchalant way I said, *"You feel sorry for her, don't you?"* He looked at me and paused for a second, then he said, *"Yes, yes I do."* I said, *"Don't. She is right where she wants to be and she is getting paid to do this job. Do not feel sorry for her. She knows what she is doing."*

In the weeks following this conversation more darkness was exposed. When I told him I was going to drive to the terminal to see what was causing the delay in his getting home, he forbade my going there. **That was a red flag!**

I let him know that I knew things were not on the up and up, but he denied any wrongdoing. I did a lot of praying. One day he phoned me from the highway. God had been dealing with him and the conviction got to him. He said he had a confession to make. I wondered why he did not wait and confess to my face, whatever this was about. He said that he had been phoning her on the company's 800 number. But, he said, they just talked.

I knew how little time he spent on the phone with me, his wife, so I was not a happy camper at all. Yet he did confess, so God asked me to forgive him. I did, with God's help. Trust had been broken though, and I knew it would take time for it to be rebuilt. That hurt a lot. Being betrayed is not fun. Knowing he had such a strong emotional connection with her and had willingly opened the door to sin was further compounded by the fact that she was young enough to be his daughter!

**Lust is no respecter of age.** Opening the door to sin is like stepping into quicksand with both feet. When you play, you pay—a worldly expression, but so true when you look at it spiritually. The Bible says that, " ... *the wages of sin is death, but the gift of God is eternal life through Jesus Christ our Lord,"* (Romans 6:23). Sin was bringing death to our marriage. Yet I could not afford the luxury of being bitter because that would hurt me more than it would anyone else. I had to forgive. Simple fact.

At first I wanted Clint to quit his job. He had quit for a lot less reason many times before, but he would not quit this time. That made it more difficult for me to believe he was letting go of her. How much was I to believe when he said they only talked? I knew they had opportunity to be alone for hours each time he returned to the truck terminal.

He often made a point of returning when she was on shift. I gave him the benefit of the doubt. For him to make that phone call to me showed me God was really dealing with him. I had to be thankful for positive change in his heart. It was a good thing, even though the news was heartbreaking. Often when there is change, there is pain. However, along with it there is gain if the change is orchestrated by God.

Several months later Clint's company had a Christmas banquet. It was the only time all year when we went out socially to something special, and I really looked forward to it. We walked into a room of a few hundred people, and she and her husband were at a table with others but had saved seats for us. *"How convenient,"* I thought. I saw red. I stopped in my tracks and told my husband, *"I am not sitting with her."* He said, *"Okay, we can sit right here."* I wanted to turn and go home, not sit anywhere; yet that would give her satisfaction, and he would probably take me home and then go back.

Then I felt a nudge from inside and knew God was challenging me to face fear, not to run. I told myself as I sucked in a big breath, **"I am not fleeing. Darkness has to flee, not light."** So we sat at the table and God even exalted me in the midst of it all. When you are hurting the most and leaning on the Lord, God can move and use you for His glory. He did, although much to my dismay. (I'm just being honest.)

I had taken a poem I had read to show to my husband's boss because it was a tribute to truckers' wives and I had not ever read anything like it. I gave it to him in case he wanted to share it during the evening. In a few minutes he came over to me and asked me to read it at the dinner. That was the last thing I wanted to do, to stand up there at the head table and face everyone with my heart breaking and my one evening out with my husband already ruined … but God had opened a door and I knew He would give me grace, so I agreed to read it.

God always goes before men and prepares the way. I had told Him years before that I would not push doors open. He would have to open them for me and lead me in with favor. So He made a way for the poem to be read. People were encouraged and I was relieved it was over. (... or so I thought!)

I proceeded to leave the platform. It was not well lit behind the head table, so I stepped carefully toward end of the platform where there were several stairs to descend. **Suddenly a man's hand reached out and grabbed me firmly by the leg! It was the CEO!!!** I stopped in my tracks and thought my heart would jump out of my mouth! Talk about shocked. To think he would do such a thing, and in front of all of those people!

I was at the top of several stairs and tried not to fall forward. When I looked down I saw that my ankle had gotten entangled in the microphone cord and it would have tripped me. That is why he grabbed my leg. He was trying to prevent an accident. (As if I had not had enough excitement for the evening!) You can be sure I just wanted to get out of that place and walk the ten miles home if necessary, even in the winter. I was on such an adrenaline high by then I probably could have done so, but the night was not over.

My husband was seated near the platform, but he could not see the cord around my foot and wanted to know what happened. I guess he didn't like it when someone reached for me, but when the shoe was on the other foot, he thought it was okay. I recognized the work of the enemy. He tries hardest to hit you with something when you are very high or very low. **My emotions were rocking, but God managed to keep me in check.**

I stood my ground and did not give the enemy the satisfaction of retreating. Not only did I stay, I made it to the mountaintop because God was working *Romans 8:28* in my behalf. Being able to uplift Jesus and help truckers' wives see His viewpoint through the poem was a bright light in the midst of much darkness. It is all about Jesus and not about me anyway. I had to lay my life down and pick up my cross. The Bible states that, "*He must increase,* but I must decrease," (*John* 3:30). Self is not to be in the center. Jesus belongs in the center.

More months passed and I saw a pattern unfold that did not make me happy. I had forgiven Clint and given him the benefit of the doubt. I thought trust was being rebuilt. He came home very late again from the terminal and I sensed something was wrong. I asked him what time he had arrived back at the truck yard. We talked a bit and the woman's name came up. I saw red because I knew he was lying to me again.

He went to bed, but I phoned her at work. I told him he'd better pray her story coincided with his, because if it didn't he would have to quit his job or I would be gone. He heard me on the phone with her. I confronted her and let her know he was listening and that her story had better be the same as his or her husband would be the next person I would call. She was so nervous she could hardly talk.

I asked her some questions, and after she answered I told her that was not at all what he had told me. I spoke firmly and boldly, not out of control, but as a woman taking charge of a volatile situation and determined to put the ungodly fire out. She backed down knowing that the sin had been exposed. I told her that he would be quitting his job, and I discerned her disappointment. I hung up and headed for the bedroom.

My husband had the covers up to his chin and had heard one side of the conversation. I told him he had a choice to make—quit his job and sever his ties with her, or I would leave and I would call her husband. He yelled something that surprised me so much. He said, *"I can't even have a friend!"* I said, *"No, not another woman communing with you when I am your wife!"* Then he actually cried. He shook and cried like a baby. Not tears of repentance, but that he had been caught and there would be a price to pay. He quit his job.

This is how people can get emotionally entangled. Their mind is under attack, and if such people are not rooted and grounded in the Word of God they will succumb to the emotions. It feeds a man's ego to have a woman show an interest in him, whether he is married or single.

That was why the Lord taught me that, as a wife, it was not proper for me to give personal comments to another man. I was to save them for my husband, so I did. The same applied for him; he was not to tell another woman that he liked her dress, for example. **It only takes a spark to get a fire going. The choices we make each day are what shape our lives.**

I was not being bombarded by men making passes at me, and I knew why. I was committed to my husband and did not entertain any fleeting moments of flirting or any such behavior with any men, especially when my husband withheld sex (which was not scriptural). I stayed faithful to him. I did not want to be vulnerable, so I just gave my desires over to the Lord and asked Him to give me grace, and He did. Plus I knew I was responsible for what thoughts I chose to entertain. So I did my best to protect my mind, my eyes, and my ears from spiritual defilement.

**People know when they look in your eyes if you are game or not. That is why I had no problem. I would not compromise, and that saved me a lot of heartache in that department.** I know what it is to have a man look at me with admiration as he appreciates a woman. That is fine. It is far different than a lustful, clothes-removing, defiling stare. Praise God for making me the lady that I am.

Even in an unhappy marriage I was glad to be a woman, a Godly woman! I know who I am in Christ. That is what keeps me pressing onward and upward rather than dwelling on circumstances. Again, the choices we make each day are the reasons we are where we are today too, folks! I am happy to say I have made some serious decisions recently that needed to be made years ago, but better late than never.

The more I get written in this book the higher I get, because when I finish writing about just some of the pain I experienced, it will be more than a new chapter for me. It will be a new book; it will be a new lifestyle; it will be a new makeover so to speak. Because this lady blossoms into the career God has been preparing her for all along. *"And we know that all things work together for good to them that love God, to them who are the called according to his purpose,"* (Romans 8:28).

It is awesome the doors He has opened for me and the new path He has positioned me on. *Galatians 6:9* is one of my favorite verses. *"And let us not be weary in well doing for in due season we shall reap if we faint not."* When this book is done it is harvest time for me. If I could shout from the rooftop without falling off I would do it! WHOOPPEE!!! Glory to God!!!!!!!

Okay, back to the grindstone for now, though. I have suffered, yes, but for sure I have never suffered one degree as much as Jesus did for me. For sure I have never sweat drops of blood. I have never had nails driven in my hands and feet, or had my side pierced, or had a crown of thorns jammed into my scalp, or suffered thirty-nine stripes on my back. I can only be humbled when I think of all that Jesus did for me at Calvary. He paid the price for me to be free and totally whole—spirit, soul, and body. He did it all (*1 Peter 2:24*).

I made a choice to climb up higher and avail myself of what He paid the price for me to have because I am a joint heir with Jesus Christ (*Romans 8:17*), and I don't like getting shortchanged by the enemy. Sometimes the enemy is ignorance, lack of knowledge, or pride. I want to bask in the presence of Jesus 24/7.

He is there all the time anyway, so I want to become more aware of His presence and praise Him more and sing songs that uplift His Name. In doing so, He simultaneously lifts my spirit and I am strengthened in Him. *John 12:32* says, *"And I, if I be lifted up from the earth, will draw all men unto me."*

It is great to hang out with Jesus. He really is cool, no matter what your age. He always understands your heart. Besides, if you are a Christian, He is closer to you than the problem is because He is in your heart, by faith. *Colossians 1:27* talks about, *"Christ in you, the hope of glory,"* so why not have fellowship continually. He's a great listener too.

Well, now it is time to learn a bit more about how control, manipulation, jealousy, fear, and intimidation can affect you adversely, if you allow them to continue. Boundaries are so necessary.

# 12. A UNIQUE TWIST

THIS CHAPTER IS UNIQUELY DIFFERENT. RATHER than sharing about a specific incident, God is leading me to search my mental filing cabinet for some specific flashbacks regarding manipulation and control. The first thing that comes to mind is the way our lives changed after we got a Miniature Schnauzer that we named Dan. At first it was rather like when there is a new addition to the family. He became our focal point and we couldn't do enough for him. It mattered not what or how many messes he made. We made excuses for him and continued to train and enjoy our new pet. Then things started to change.

I started to notice that whenever Clint would get upset with me he would quickly turn to Dan for affection and would focus on him. It didn't seem to be a big deal at the time, so although I was aware I didn't fuss about it much. More time passed and I noticed Clint would get upset when I tried to discipline the dog. He would not let me train him. If Dan made a mess and I wanted to discipline him, my husband stopped the discipline. Soon the dog learned who had control and he took over doing his own thing. And guess who had to clean it up? Me.

Clint went to work for a week or so at a time so I took those opportunities to discipline Dan. Then Clint would come home and let the dog do his own thing. When Clint was home he would feed Dan scraps from the dinner table and let him drag dog treats into any room of the house to eat then or leave for later. You can be sure the dog never ran out of food or treats no matter how tight the budget.

Clint was off work ill for four months and finances were so tight that I couldn't get my prescription filled or get my hair trimmed, but Dan went to the groomer twice and had lots of food and treats in the cupboard. Kind of gives a woman a message!

If that message wasn't loud and clear enough, the dog then started sleeping in the master bedroom, no longer at the foot of the bed but in the middle between me and my husband, on top of the covers. I protested loudly, to no avail. God heard and knew the priorities were out of order. He intervened. He used a pastor to speak a word saying that when you have to let the dog sleep with you, and sometimes under the covers, that is sick. The congregation groaned. I said, *"Amen!"* in agreement, as did many others. My husband's reaction was different. He took offense. He decided it was time to change churches again.

When a person is going contrary to God's will and plan, God will give him or her a warning, and then another. If the individual will not yield, God will rebuke him or her publicly. He will make the sin public knowledge. I believe the shame should cause the guilty party to repent. In Clint's case, he did not repent. He took offense and hardened his heart against the pastor and was therefore unable to receive from him. Sure enough, we moved on to yet another church.

My thinking did not line up with scripture. Submitting to my husband did not mean I was to submit if what he was doing was sin. That put me in sin too. He left in rebellion against the pastor, and my following in his footsteps put me in rebellion as well. God did not call me to submit to my husband if it meant I would be in sin. I needed to draw the line but lacked understanding of the Bible. It is dangerous to be ignorant.

The Bible says, *"My people are destroyed for lack of knowledge: because thou hast rejected knowledge, I will also reject thee..."* (Hosea 4:6). Also, 2 Timothy 2:15 says, *"Study to shew thyself approved unto God, a workman that needeth not to be ashamed, rightly dividing the word of truth."* This told me I had some responsibility to make sure my life lined up with the Word of God, and that I was not to take things for granted. Even when a leader of a flock was teaching, I was not to accept everything automatically because it was told to me by a leader.

God calls all of us to be accountable for ourselves. I needed to be sure that anyone I followed was not in error and to make an effort to stay in truth. The bottom line is, I should have stayed at the church and let my husband run if he wanted to. A pastor told me this after the fact, and I never forgot it.

As for the dog, I gave my husband an ultimatum: sleep with me or with the dog, not both. It was the beginning of the end. He slept with me but worried so much about the dog that if he thought Dan was cold he would get up at any hour and cover him and never complain about it. If a human being needed to be pampered a bit in the wee hours, Clint's attitude was considerably less charitable. So, an animal that was meant to be a blessing and a watchdog for me was being used to cause division in our family.

Satan's ways are subtle; deception is gradual. The door was opened when my husband would not allow me to discipline the dog, and that opened the way for more things to get out of order. Kind of like stepping into quicksand, and in no time the gradual sinking, smothering process takes place. If the dog decided to use the carpet for a bathroom, Clint would not let me correct him.

When someone came to the door, Dan would bark continuously. If you picked him up he growled and bared his teeth so that even I would not pick him up. As more time without correction went on, I saw Dan's attitude change. He became more like my husband—always upset.

It reminds me of what happens when parents disagree on how to discipline the children. That causes an open door for the enemy to begin sowing discord. *Luke 11:17* says, "*... Every kingdom divided against itself is brought to desolation; and a house divided against a house falleth.*" When parents disagree on discipline, the children know and it is not long before they begin to play one parent against the other. At least the dog wasn't smart enough to do that ... at first.

So what do you do when something like this happens? To do nothing would allow the problem to escalate. I wanted to send the dog to training camp but Clint refused. I did what I could when I was home alone with him, but the real problem was that Clint was putting Dan before me. The enemy used those wrong priorities to open the wedge further in our marriage.

Soon the dog was the only one getting lots of hugs and attention when Clint got home from work after a week on the road. Again, kind of gives a woman a message. Clint believed that the dog loved him unconditionally, but I told him that if Dan could talk it would be a different story. The first time Dan said something Clint didn't agree with, he would abandon the dog.

So by now my marriage consisted of a husband who gave the dog more attention than he gave me; a husband who refused to let me do his laundry and now was refusing to even dine with me. He wanted to learn to cook his own meals and chose to eat alone. We went to church in separate cars. He quit mowing the lawn as well as doing odd jobs around the home. He came and went as he pleased. When he was done work, it did not mean he came home.

Once he had been gone three days. When he came home he went to visit friends in town and then went back to the truck without even coming home that night at all. He did this more than once. He was denying me intimacy. He stopped phoning long distance. He had shut down emotionally and simply would not even try to have a conversation that was anything more than superficial. Our marriage was dying, if not already dead. But I still believed God could heal it, so I kept praying.

One night I awoke, as I had many times before, to feel my husband's fists hitting me. He was having another nightmare. He would not usually awaken until after he had flailed around wildly for some time, hitting me in the back or shoulder or back of my head. Then I would hear him say, **"Did I hit you?"** and I would tell him what happened. I had learned to sleep pretty lightly when he was home because of these nightmares, and I had learned to move pretty quickly to get out of bed before I got hit. Sometimes, though, the sheets would entangle me and I wouldn't get out of the way fast enough.

One of those times he awoke and I was crying because he had hit me with his fist. I was in pain and I was afraid. He said he was sorry and broke down saying, *"What kind of a monster am I?"* It was because of rare moments like this I stayed. I knew he was so mixed up inside, and I kept praying for him. God wanted him free too.

Finally, though, it seemed the tables turned. He was apparently having another nightmare, but I was in such a sound sleep that night that my reflexes kicked in and I started punching him!! I woke up and found that he was already awake and was very upset that I was punching him!! From that time on he slept in another bedroom. He couldn't take it, not even once, but I had endured it on and off for years.

So now we did not sleep together, dine together, or drive to church together. He wouldn't let me do his laundry or cook for him, and all my efforts to be a helpmeet to him were denied. My offer was there, but he denied the offer. God showed me that as long as I offered, that was all that mattered from my perspective. His rejection of my help was something he would have to answer for; I was clear.

I made sure my hands were clean by continuing to offer to cook his meals, wash his clothes and generally be a help to him. I knew that God keeps a very accurate record and knows the motives of the heart. I was responsible for my behavior, as Clint was for his.

The marriage was dead, and I started to face that fact. I knew God could resurrect it, but would He? My husband had a free will and I knew God would not violate his free will. Once again, God brought forth a series of events that triggered strong reactions from my husband. When pressure is applied it does not take long to see what is really on the inside. A tree is known by its fruit.

# 13. HOMEWARD BOUND

FIVE LONG YEARS HAD PASSED SINCE I had last seen my son and his wife and my grandson in Canada. Within that time they had another son (another grandson for me!) whom I had never seen in person. I got a lot of photos through the computer, but holding that two-year-old was something I longed to do, as would any grandmother.

My daughter and her husband had been to Texas within the previous two years, but I had not seen my granddaughter for five years. Nor had I seen my three-week-old grandson. Needless to say, I was very excited about going back home. It was June and spring had sprung for sure.

Clint was not going on the trip. He had changed jobs and was not yet eligible for a vacation. He knew I was flying and said very little about it. I sensed his jealousy so I tried not to show my excitement. How sad that a person has to put water on their joy to prevent someone from expressing such jealousy.

Actually, I did not have to, but to keep peace I did. I gave in to the manipulation and walked on eggs to avoid strife. This was not good because it simply enabled his wrong behavior to continue. What is not confronted cannot be conquered.

The night before my flight was to leave, Clint left for work. He told me I could not take the car to the airport and to leave it at the house. Yet he made no arrangements for me to get to the airport. I told him I paid for the car and I needed it, and thankfully he did not argue further. I told him there was one thing I would really like from him—I wanted his blessing when I left on this trip. It had been so long since I had seen my family, and I did not want to go there with a cloud over my head because of his anger.

His verbal response was, *"Well you have my blessing. Go." "Thank you,"* I said. When it was time to go, though, it was a different story. He was leaving for work and would not give me a hug or kiss even though he knew I would fly out in the morning. He just left for work. I tried not to let the hurt get in my heart but it did hurt. Rejection hurts! He could see his kids whenever he wanted because they lived in town. In fact, if he did not see them for a month he would be in tears and very upset. But he didn't care about my desire to see my children and did nothing to help me. He refused to help plan a visit or budget for the cost, and he refused to go with me. He said he would not go back to Canada because people teased him about his accent. Again, he was taking offense and it was his loss. It hurt him a lot more than it hurt my family.

As for me, I was thrilled to get to the airport and see my son, his wife, and their oldest son there to greet me. Feeling that little boy's arms around my neck was a thrill money could not buy. His soft voice saying, **"Hi Gramma Texas,"** was music to my ears. The tears in my son's eyes said it all. His love was overflowing and it was wonderful. My daughter-in-law looked radiant as always. Her smile spoke volumes. "Family" was the word that hugged each of us in that special moment. A priceless memory indeed!

We then drove a few hours straight to my daughter's home. My nine-year-old granddaughter was sitting on the front step when we pulled up. She didn't know I was coming, and when she saw me her mouth dropped open and it was a sight to see. Her eyes popped out of her little face and her feet started to run toward me. Her hug nearly broke my neck, but it was great.

She looked so endearingly into my face and said, "Hi Grammie Texas. *Grammie Texas, you're not old, you're pretty. You are so pretty. Grammie you are so pretty!*" I knew she saw the glory of the Lord on me, and I can tell you I was one happy camper! **In just those few moments she had given me more compliments than I had received in months.**

I call that another cherished memory. Then my daughter moved quickly down the steps to greet me too. The tears in her eyes and her beautiful smile said it all. She was so happy and so was I. She had just given birth to a bouncing baby boy, and I was about to see him now for the first time. He was three weeks old. Her husband greeted me and his face showed such joy as he handed me their new son. My heart welled up with love as I looked into the face of that miracle. Every child is a miracle. It is a new life and God is the giver of life. Again, it was a priceless cherished memory.

I had not seen my son in five years though, so I joined his family and we went to his home. We pulled into his driveway and soon I saw my two-year-old grandson running toward me across the grass from the next door neighbor's home where the babysitter lived. It was my first time seeing him in person, and I did not want to overwhelm him.

I knelt down to see his face better, and to my surprise his little arms reached out towards me in a big hug, and the sweetest smile was just beaming at me from his little face. I stood up and swung him around and around. What a thrill. He had opened his little heart to me and was not holding back at all. My eyes filled with tears as love overflowed.

It was wonderful watching the two boys playing together when we went in the house—sometimes peacefully, sometimes not, but boys will be boys. We had a great time of reminiscing. Everyone needs family. I needed them and they needed me.

The next day they took me to stay at my daughter's home. I was in the house only about ten minutes when the phone rang. It was my husband calling from Texas. I took the call, wondering what was wrong because I did not expect to hear from him since he wouldn't even kiss me goodbye. It didn't take long to find out what he wanted.

He said, *"I just called to tell you I want a divorce."* It hit me like a brick. I calmly said, *"That's fine with me."* He said, *"So you might as well stay up there. You don't have to come back. I'll just sell everything and ship the rest to you. I tore up our wedding pictures too."* I told him I was enjoying time with family and would talk to him when I got home; that I would come home when I was done my visit, and then I ended the call. Truly God gave me courage and grace. But then the grieving started.

My heart hurt so much. For two days I could not do anything. I just rested and cried, and my daughter and I had a special time of bonding. I had so looked forward to seeing friends and relatives I had not seen for so long

But suddenly, I felt like the wind had been knocked out of me. I did not want to see anyone and have to pretend all was well in Texas. I was not prepared to do that after all the mental pressure I had been under. I really needed this vacation and rest, not more stress.

The phone rang again. This time God used a very good friend of mine to invite me to a Bible study she was having that night. I told her what had happened and we prayed together. I knew I should go to the meeting but did not say anything about the call from my husband to the others there. I forced myself to get ready. I was battling oppression and depression. Despite all I went through, depression was never something I had to deal with in myself. But there was a lot being said against me in Texas and there was power in those words.

At that moment I was not entering into spiritual warfare like I needed to. Thank God for intercessors, and thank God for all the time I had spent interceding for others; that was now a harvest for me when I needed prayer. "*What goes around, comes around,*" is how the world says it. I say God will not be indebted to anyone, ever. I sow prayer for others, with expectation of a harvest. It is the sowing and reaping principle, not greed (*Galatians 6:7-9*).

The Bible study went well; I saw people I had not seen in five years and some in ten years, so it was a blessing and I was glad I went. Women from several churches met once a month. God knew I needed His touch, and He used people at that meeting to uplift my spirit. Looking into the eyes of someone who has the joy of the Lord does wonders to uplift a person.

After that I spent the rest of my time with my children and my brother and sister-in-law and just a few friends. The time went quickly, but it was wonderful to be with family. I did not look forward to what I would face when I returned home to Texas. I tried not to think about it because I did not know if things had been smashed, literally, or if the wedding photos had been destroyed, or if it had just been an empty threat. Remember what I wrote earlier about how the enemy, satan, attacks the hardest when you are really down or on a real spiritual high. Well, I was on a high seeing two of my grandchildren for the first time ever, not to mention seeing everyone else too.

I think one of the hardest things I ever did was get back on that plane and leave Canada. I cried for ninety minutes; the tears just kept dripping and the stewardess just kept bringing me more tissue. I had long since quit caring what other people thought about me. I just let the tears flow. At least I had all three seats to myself. That was a first.

Back home in Texas I pulled into the driveway, and much to my surprise my husband was home. I was surprised because about ten weeks before I left on my trip to Canada he had moved out of the house into a small storage building on our property. He lived there when he wasn't on the road. Before I left for Canada I had the locks changed, but he had apparently forced the door frame and gained entry into the house.

So, I walked into the house and he was just walking from the bathroom across the living-room, butt naked except for a towel. He heard the dog barking and was looking out the window to see my car when I greeted him from inside the house!

I asked him where the divorce papers were so I could sign them. He did not have any divorce papers; he had simply made a threat. No action followed. I told him I would be glad to turn the tables, and since he did not file, I would. Enough was enough. It was very difficult preparing mentally for a divorce and for moving out, then returning to learn it was only an empty threat. I went outside and sat in the car and locked the doors, deciding to wait there until he left.

He came out and tried to talk to me. I opened the window just an inch or so, then told him, **"Don't you know I am AFRAID of you?** *I am not opening my window so you can smash me in the face. I thought we could agree on what to* *do with things and it would be a lot less costly, but I guess that is impossible with you.*" He looked like a little boy who was quite startled. It was amazing that this would be news to him after all the abuse.

In about ten minutes we agreed on what to do with everything. I waited until he left and then went inside. As I was carrying in my luggage, it was a relief to see he had not smashed anything. He really had torn up all our wedding photos though. I still find it amazing that a man could do such a thing. However, God restores and I had taken our favorite wedding photo to Canada. That is love; regardless of how he was treating me, I was determined to do the right thing before God. In fact, I even brought him a little gift from Canada too. Love turns away anger.

I did not have enough money to do anything about my situation at that time, and when I did have the finances I just couldn't do it. I was prepared mentally for a divorce, but I just couldn't do it. Why not? Because in my heart I needed a release from God and I did not have revelation of certain scriptures that I needed. So what did God do? He lovingly gave me grace, protected me, and between that June and the following April I received the understanding of the scriptures that I needed to get the release from God. I received an answer to an email I wrote to a Christian ministry. The letter enlightened me with certain scriptures and helped me a lot. Yet I waited for confirmation as to what I was to do, if anything.

From that time in June until December there was a complete breakdown in communication as my husband just came and went as he pleased. He did not know what it was to be committed to me, or to God, or to a home church, or to a job. He lacked commitment in every area of his life.

Consequently, I was isolated a lot. He would not take me with him when he visited his children. He was jealous of any attention they showed me. He would visit them directly after work or at another time. I finally decided I didn't have to beg to have a relationship with anyone and accepted that God was protecting me.

One couple we knew was not comfortable around me because of the anointing that was on me. Words were not necessary. They knew I would not compromise in the things of the Lord. It is sin for unwed Christians to live together outside of marriage. I did not condemn, nor did I condone their relationship, and they knew it. I was not the one that was uncomfortable. I recognized that I was not fighting flesh and blood. It was a spiritual battle. Light and darkness just do not mix. *Ephesians 6:12* says, *"For we wrestle not against flesh and blood but against principalities, against powers, against the rulers of the darkness of this world, against spiritual wickedness in high places."*

Thanksgiving came and Clint told me not to plan anything. In other words, he did not want me to invite his family. He told me his daughter had to work that day anyway. So I did nothing. A few days prior to Thanksgiving she phoned asking what time they were to come for Thanksgiving dinner. I told her I had not planned anything because her dad had told me not to. He had told me she was working.

She informed me she was only working half the day and could come at 1 p.m. So I agreed to prepare dinner. She brought dessert and Clint was agitated. He did not like it when I would do something for family. Rather than be happy to have family get together he was very uptight, very antisocial.

It was so disheartening to hear the conversation turn from praising God to criticism, condemnation and strife. I tried to set the tone by having everyone give a praise report for something the Lord had done for them in the last year. We did, and that part was great, but soon critical words came forth as my husband criticized and condemned me. He continued and I was grieved that he did this in front of the grandchildren.

He also made a point of bringing up his late wife twice in an effort to upset me, but I said nothing. (Our pastor had counseled Clint that to do so was in very poor taste, yet he kept trying to needle me.) He seemed so disappointed when I did not bite the bullet. God had taught me how to recognize the enemy and hold up my shield of faith, and it worked. My husband's words were darts that I learned to resist silently by using my shield of faith. The silence resulted in his being embarrassed because he was not successful in creating strife. It was the last time his family came to our home.

Instead, he would visit their homes himself, and he proceeded to plant a lot of seeds against me, lying both to them and to me as well. Compulsive lying is so damaging. It got to the point that they no longer wanted a relationship with me. The same thing happened with an elderly couple from the church. God showed me I didn't have to answer for their attitude, just for mine, so I decided to enjoy my new home (we had purchased a new double-wide mobile home) and make the best of it. I cleaned as unto the Lord, I rejoiced and praised Him, but I was longing for family.

I went to Bible school full time and worked full time, so it was not like I sat around feeling sorry for myself. My husband was not home during the week anyway, so I put my evening hours to good use. At the end of the first semester I had four A's and my self-esteem started to rise. God is good!

Abusive behavior has a way of crushing your esteem. I knew who I was "in Christ," but my personal esteem was shattered. The last thing my husband wanted to do was give me a compliment, because his self-esteem was so low. There was no nurturing at all. He abandoned me in many ways.

He controlled our sexual relationship too. He withheld sex from me on and off for years. This kind of control is a form of witchcraft. He enjoyed the manipulation. In a counseling session with our pastor, I told him that I was not being abused sexually but that we had stopped having sex. He said, "*Withholding sex from your mate is a form of witchcraft.*" Yet it continued.

That which was to be something beautiful and blessed by God became merely having sex, which is far different from lovemaking. Eventually he loved the manipulation and control more than lovemaking. The relationship deteriorated from love making ... to having sex ... to control by withholding sex ... which is a form of witchcraft. Yet he had no aversion to self-gratification.

Self-centeredness is the opposite of God's way. Lust is the devil's counterfeit of the real thing. God is the Source of unconditional love. Making love God's way is intimate, pure, and fulfilling. God's ways really do satisfy. The devil's thrills are temporary; he's got nothing good that lasts. That line is in a song I wrote called, *A Happy Backslider?* Please note there is a question mark at the end of the title because there is no such thing as a happy backslider. Their life is nothing but hell on earth. But I've got Good News—Jesus hasn't ever given up on anyone. His love draws everyone closer and His love always breaks through.

A Christ-centered marriage between a man and a woman is the only institution in which God blesses the sexual relationship; and God knows how to bless! When it comes to being intimate, He's the Master because He is our Creator and He does all things well.

The Holy Ghost is a perfect teacher of students whose hearts' desire is to please God. One cannot please God without being pleased himself or herself. He will not leave anyone shortchanged. The devil cannot hold a candle to what God has for His children who will trust Him completely. God is not a prude.

I did not plan on getting into all of that, but I believe someone needed to know it. My thirteen years of being single following salvation helped me to crucify the flesh when our marriage was attacked in this area. Again, God works it all together for good according to *Romans 8:28*. Nothing I go through is ever in vain. As I trust God, each situation becomes a stepping stone, not a stumbling block. What the devil means for evil, God turns around for good.

Whether I was 'homeward bound' to Canada or to the USA there was much heartache in both places. It was a very deep valley and there seemed to be no light at the end of the tunnel, yet I knew God was with me, because the Lord always keeps His promises—always! And I was so glad because I was about to face death head on and I needed His help big time!

# 14. DEATH KNOCKS

ON ANOTHER OCCASION, A FEW YEARS later, I was able to fly back to Canada for a Christmas-time visit that proved to be life threatening. For months I was able to enjoy the plans I had for Christmas. My boss had given me a return flight to Ontario, Canada and I was going to be with my family at Christmas for the first time in ten years! It brought a lift to my spirit just thinking about it. I told my husband that he was invited, but he said he wouldn't fly. Fear. He was going to spend Christmas in town with his children.

Before I go any further I want to point out something. If I had not obeyed the Holy Spirit by accepting a new job that paid less, I would not have received that free flight ticket. My flesh was not too happy with the pay cut, but I knew to trust God as my Source, not my paycheck.

God had a plan, and my obedience set me up for blessings. *Isaiah 1:19* says, *"If ye be willing and obedient, ye shall eat the good of the land."* At Christmas I was given the free flight ticket. After five months' employment the store was sold, and I also received two weeks' paid vacation.

Being a workaholic is not God's way to get ahead. I had favor with God and with my Christian employer, thankfully. There was one other time when the Lord redirected me away from what I thought was the perfect job for me. I share to help you learn the importance of hearing the voice of the Holy Spirit and being sensitive to the inner witness he gives. He will confirm His leading. *"My sheep hear my voice, and I know them, and they follow me,"* (*John 10:27*).

Before moving to Texas, I had been employed in a high end shoe store for one year. One day I received a phone call letting me know I was accepted for a certain government office position that paid very well. I was thrilled to get the job (I had several years' office experience, so I was looking forward to returning to office work).

Before I got off the phone I realized I had no peace. In fact, I could hardly speak. So I asked the woman on the phone if I could call her back in about ten minutes. She agreed. I gathered my thoughts for a minute, walked to the back of the store, prayed, came back out and knew I had to decline the new job. I also knew it would be easier to phone and get it over with immediately, because the longer I waited the more I would be tempted not to phone. I obeyed the Lord and made the call.

About an hour passed, and I still did not have peace about what I had done. I was fuming. It would have been so nice to earn that kind of money, but I had chosen to obey the Lord, so at the very least I figured I should feel good about it. Soon I marched to the back of the store again, and this time I had a little talk with Jesus—a very serious talk.

I was straightforward because He sees my heart anyway. I said, *"Lord, if I did the right thing in not taking that high paying job, then why aren't I happy?!!"* Immediately I heard a strong, loving voice say, **"Because the FLESH dies hard!"** How true. How very true. Ouch! Ouchy!! *"He must increase, but I must decrease,"* (John 3:30). I also had to remember that God is my Source, not my paycheck. *"But my God shall supply all your need according to his riches in glory by Christ Jesus,"* (Philippians 4:19).

I was so glad I obeyed though, because as it turned out, the next job was to stand in the gap for the assistant manager of a Christian bookstore. He was quite ill, so I got to work in the store for a few months by myself. God kept opening doors, and I walked through them gaining experience in different areas. I was learning as well as assisting others; giving and receiving. The Lord was keeping me in balance.

The Lord kept me there for three months with no vehicle and little money. However, He faithfully provided a place for me to stay with my own big bedroom, all meals provided, plus I got to bond with three wonderful Christians. They taught me a lot about unconditional love. Without a doubt, obeying God and putting your trust in Him is the best way. Man's plan may be good, but God's plan is always far better. He is able to do "… *exceeding abundantly above all that we ask or think, according to the power that worketh in us,*" (Ephesians 3:20).

Experiences taught me that trusting God was something I had to do whether I lived in Canada or the USA. Little did I know I would have more opportunities to trust God when the plane took off. After making one stop I learned we could not continue from there to Canada because of mechanical problems, and because another plane was overbooked by forty people. So the airline put me up at a good hotel—at their expense, including the meals—and rebooked my flight for early the next morning.

*Romans 8:28* kicked into action because the rib-eye dinner and home-made cheesecake were superb. Another female passenger and I got a room next to each other, and we enjoyed the best meal I'd had in years. It was a special evening, even though we had to rise early the next morning. The next leg of the journey proved less time-consuming, even though there were large crowds and bad weather. In fact, we had to wait for the flight to arrive. It was the first flight allowed to fly out due to bad weather.

My daughter and my son-in-law had arranged for a sitter while they drove to pick me up at the airport. Due to eight inches of new snow, they left early and were already at the airport when I learned my flight was canceled. They decided to get a hotel and stay. God worked it out so they had two sitters taking turns. All our needs were met.

Thank God for cell phones. After dinner my daughter and I spoke to each other from our respective hotels. When I told her mine was paid for and that there was a sofa, table, chairs, sink, coffee pot, fridge, microwave, and two beds, she said, "*Okay Mom, that's enough, let's just say our motel is not like that at all.*" Then she laughed. I told her I even had a package of micro-wave popcorn in my luggage (just in case).

We laughed and had a fun visit, and I assured her I would be on that plane the next day. She had to leave the motel at 11 a.m. and I did not arrive until 4:30 p.m. When I finally found her and my son-in-law she was jumping up and down like a pogo stick and it tickled my heart. What a thrill to see your own child after two years.

We enjoyed a wonderful dinner together, then made it to their home that evening. It had been a long time since I left my Canadian home, but we made it safely, and that was all that really mattered. I had less than a week to visit, and this delay cut into my time, so I was wondering how to manage seeing everyone. Little did I know there was yet another big surprise waiting, as well as another delay.

Man can make his plans, but that does not mean it will be done that way. I found that out the day before Christmas. Relatives picked me up and took me to someone's house in the country. I knew some of the people there, and we had a traditional Christmas dinner. After returning to town I arrived at my daughter's home around 8:30 p.m. I told her my tummy didn't feel good; I figured I must have eaten too much. The children were sleeping when she and her husband went to visit family for an hour.

I told them I was fine, took an antacid and was sure I would be okay. They left. I was not okay. The antacid did nothing, so I took something else. No change. Then up came my dinner. I thought for sure I would feel better after I rested a bit. Not so. I paced the floor, felt shaky and weak, so I took the cordless phone to the bedroom along with the phone number they had left for me.

I rested for a bit, and when I started having trouble breathing I realized I could not even use the phone, let alone see the phone number. I prayed, *"God, what is wrong with me? I should feel better by now. Please help me."* He spoke to my heart so calmly and reassuringly and said, *"It is okay, I have nudged your daughter and she is on her way."* It was such a relief.

Just for the record, the Bible does say, *"Call unto me and I will answer thee,"* (*Jeremiah 33:3*). I called and He answered. It is very scriptural, praise God.

In just moments I heard the front door and their voices. They called 911 and the ambulance was on its way. I passed out, and when I came to my son-in-law was trying to get me to come around as he held me in a sitting position. I kept hearing him ask me if I could hear him. Then my eyes opened, and my first thoughts were, **"Who is this man ... and in my face ... ?!"** Then in a moment I realized who he was, but before I could speak I passed out again. I remember hearing the ambulance attendant's voice and I could almost feel his adrenaline. Mine sure wasn't kicking in—I could hardly breathe. I heard him say that my blood pressure was something over forty-eight, and I knew I was in trouble. I passed out again. It wasn't denial either!

Long story short, they thought they were going to have to use the paddles. They had them ready, but I managed to come around, so they put me in the ambulance. It just happened to be 25 degrees below zero (Fahrenheit), and there I was in my short tiger print gown under the open sky. The wheels of the stretcher bumped because of the snow, and I was afraid I would fall off. I called out to my daughter and was so relieved when she grabbed my hand and told me that she was coming with me. I couldn't open my eyes, but it helped me relax.

To say the least I was very ill. The hospital called for the crash cart and I heard the doctor say, *"Looks like an overdose."* I didn't have the strength to draw in my breath, but I would have if I could have after that remark. Then I heard his voice on the other side of the bed, and he said the same thing.

I prayed and said, *"God, will You please show that Doctor what is wrong with me because You know I DID NOT overdose!!"* Then I passed out again. My vitals stabilized after that prayer and they did not have to use the paddles. They kept the heart monitor on all night. Both of my children were there. I remember briefly seeing their solemn faces and was also aware that it was Christmas Eve. It was so upsetting for everyone.

The specialist arrived in the morning and determined that I had not had a seizure. He then verified that I had a food allergy and severe food poisoning. He said that even if no one else had gotten ill it was definitely food poisoning. This was a first for me. The only thing I remember is that I felt fine until I ate the Christmas pudding.

Later I learned there was rum in it, and my body had not had anything alcoholic for twenty-two years. It seemed incredible that this was the culprit. I learned later that no one else got ill, so what can I say? We are in a spiritual battle. *"We wrestle not against flesh and blood, but against principalities, against powers, against the rulers of the darkness of this world, against spiritual wickedness in high places,"* (Ephesians 6:12). What the devil meant for evil, God used for good.

The good news was that I could not fly home on my return date, so my visit was extended until after the New Year. That suited me just fine. It gave me time to get stronger, and each day that passed I continued to improve. I got to see lots of people and go lots of places. It was restoration. I went sleigh riding too and had a great time. Food would probably never look the same to me. I am still careful of what I eat, and I do not worry about hurting the cook's feelings if I don't like something. I just won't eat it. No doubt others would feel the same after an episode like that, not to mention the nearly $2,000 hospital bill.

My husband had medical coverage for me that came into effect through his work less than a month before this incident. He changed jobs quite often, so this was a miracle provision from God. God took care of the need. Praise the Lord. I got an extended vacation, better weather in Ontario, Canada in December and early January than they had in Texas that year. Talk about God turning things around. It was so exhilarating in the fresh air, and lots of snowplows kept the roads clear so we had no problem getting around at all. Canadians are tough. The rest of my time in Canada was spent building happy memories. I managed to get out of the hospital by noon Christmas day.

I learned that a lot of people had an unexpected change of plans at Christmas time that year. But I wonder how many people took it calmly, recognized the hand of God in the midst of it all, and even thanked Him for being there and being in charge? I know I did, and it was wonderful. When I awoke December 25 in the hospital and lifted my head off the pillow I could see out the window straight down the street. There was a large red brick house that resembled some of the homes painted by Thomas Kinkade, *Painter of Light.*

The fresh white snow lay like a peaceful blanket at eight a.m., and only one brave person was walking towards the hospital. I imagined his boots squeaking on the snow as he walked quickly and carefully because it was quite cold. It made a pretty picture in my mind and was certainly not something I expected to see from a hospital bed. God even arranged that touching moment. It is good to appreciate the small things too. It was like seeing a postcard come alive.

We arrived at the house and I was able to watch my grandchildren open their gifts. What a joy! God was bringing restoration to my life, and it was wonderful. My granddaughter was nine and I had not seen her in five years. Too-o-o-o long.

My husband had not wanted to come with me, but he did not act very happy about my extended visit. Nor did he show concern about my health. He was more concerned about the medical bill. I knew without a doubt that we had coverage. It was not a coincidence.

So I kept my joy and focused on Jesus. Clint called a few times, but I chose not to communicate long distance when he refused to communicate locally! He did not want to be with me but wanted to know when I would be home. He would not tell talk to me about anything important, such as if the pipes had frozen in our mobile home (Texas could be very cold in the winter) or if there were any other problems. It was superficial conversation, so I stood my ground and kept the call brief.

My children wanted me to move back to Canada. Tempted as I was, God called me to Texas, even though I sensed an impending divorce. I knew when I went back home to Texas it was decision time. My friends in Canada were so supportive and compassionate and offered to help in whatever way they could. It touched my heart, but I knew not to be led by emotions.

Back to the airport again, this time in the early morning hours. No traffic, great trip. Great breakfast too. Everything was lookin' good. I arrived back in Texas and friends met me at the airport. Every need was met. God is faithful. The roads were not anything to brag about, but I made it home safely. My husband was in bed sleeping and stayed in bed. I unloaded the luggage by myself, snow and all, and settled in. At least the dog greeted me.

Back to reality, rejection big time. Fend for yourself. Get your own car oil changed, but he will change the oil in his car himself. It is true there is no place like home, but my idea of home—and the home I lived in—did not in any way match. You can sense the atmosphere in a home as soon as you enter, and I sensed the sadness and gloom that lived in our house. I could not deny the truth any more.

The next four months of my life were about leaving one phase and entering something far better. God did a deep work in my heart. My husband and I were living like divorced people under one roof. Enough was finally enough!

God did not allow me to return to work. He wanted me at home. He would not allow more than I could bear. God was well aware of the mental, financial and emotional pressures. When the business I worked for was sold, my hours were cut so Clint told me to quit. I did, not knowing he had a plan. At the time, I had made every car payment from my paycheck, as promised.

When Clint had the last mental breakdown and no income for four months, we refinanced the car to reduce payments. He told me he would make the payments and that I was to quit my job. I quit. The car was repossessed within months because he did not honor his word. He implemented his plan, which left me abandoned in the country without a car. Then he moved out!

Even though I sensed God wanted me home, I knew I had financial obligations so I filled out a few job applications. When I did I also prayed like this: *"Father, I submit this application and I pray that if this job would in any way take me away from the center of your perfect will for my life, then close the door. But if it is right where you want me, then please give me favor with the employer and employees, and send Your angels to minister on my behalf, in Jesus' Name. The results are in your hands, Father."*

I got a phone call and was interviewed by several people for an office job at a maximum security prison. Since the job was for afternoons, and I only found that out when I was interviewed, I requested time to let my husband know and told them I would call them Monday. They told me to let them know which job I wanted (there were two available). On Monday I phoned and let them know which job I wanted. The next step was for them to call me and tell me when to start, after my paperwork was processed.

I was happy about getting the job and told friends. Three days later I phoned to see why they had not called me yet, and they told me they were still interviewing. That was a shock to me. I told them I thought I got the job. Not so, they said, they were still interviewing. Pretty humbling, but that was okay. I wanted God's will to be done. In a few days I received a letter in the mail letting me know I did not get the job. It hurt.

God knew I needed a special word to help me understand, so He spoke to me directly through a pastor on television. He did not say these exact words, but very close: **"God has the bird's eye viewpoint. His prevention is your protection. There are some things you don't know about the situation. You dared to pray that dangerous prayer, 'If it be Thy will.' "**

It was not a coincidence. I knew God had spoken to my heart through that pastor, and it helped me a lot. It was a Divine encounter. Praise the Lord for Christian television.

This just made me all the more certain that I was right where God wanted me to be. I felt His hand upon me. It was like I couldn't go anywhere else to apply for a job. I was happy to be home. I had worked full time for several years and was in my fifties. Being home and off my feet was just fine with me. I knew God had a plan. He also knew the danger I was in because of all the denial, stress, abuse and fatigue. I returned home to discover Clint had removed my name from our bank accounts. He said I hadn't done anything wrong, but he believed he could do better.

So, he removed my name and would not put it back on when I protested. It was a black mark against me. I was so shocked. I did not know anyone could do such a thing. Ignorance is costly. I sensed a third party advised him on this and reminded myself that no matter what happens, God is my Source. This black mark made me look bad but God knew the truth and that comforted me. *Matthew 5:10-12 reads, "Blessed are they which are persecuted for righteousness sake: for theirs is the kingdom of heaven. Blessed are ye, when men shall revile you, and persecute you, and shall say all manner of evil against you falsely, for my sake, Rejoice and be exceeding glad: for great is your reward in heaven: for so persecuted they the prophets which were before you."*

Clint wanted to control, so I let go of managing the finances. It was good to be free of the responsibility after nearly eleven years. He had never been home long enough to deal with the finances, nor did he ever want to. Until now it seemed.

So, my husband controlled the finances, the sex (there wasn't any most of the time), and now I had no transportation. He had three vehicles but only two were operable. He used one for work and refused to give me the keys for the other. I was grounded, and we lived in a rural area. He was away from Sunday night or Monday morning until Friday night or Saturday morning every week. Prior to that he had come home more frequently. Nevertheless, God met my need. One phone call and I had arranged for a ride to church regularly. Praise the Lord. **Man kept throwing up roadblocks and God just lifted me up above them. I was blessed!**

Oops ... forgot to tell you that when I reached bottom, after nearly a month of having no job, no money, no car, no companionship and no communion with my husband (except for verbal abuse), in desperation I searched the Internet for information on emotional abuse. I hit pay dirt!

I found a book about emotional abuse. I ordered it, and on Valentine's Day it arrived at the bookstore. I had just enough money to purchase it, so I picked it up, brought it home and started reading. It talked about overcoming destructive patterns and reclaiming yourself. At that point in my life, the real me had been virtually snuffed out because my identity was wrapped up in my husband. I no longer had a life. I did nothing for me. I had no interests any more, no respect.

I remember the clerk's face when he handed me my change after reading the title. He was especially kind. He probably did not know it, but I really appreciated the kindness and compassion he showed me. The book was my Valentine's Day gift from the Lord. He knows how to heal hearts. He knows when we need understanding and enlightenment.

I started to read and soon learned it was not a book I would read quickly. **Something happened on the inside of me as I read. It was as if the lights were coming on. Something deep inside was happening. Truth was coming forth and I knew it. The more I dug in, the more I wanted to. Tears came and I suffered pain as God did spiritual surgery on me.** I was reading this book when the phone rang. A Christian friend invited me for a complimentary eight-day stay at her bed and breakfast, transportation provided.

One day I wrote a poem about the work God did in me while I was a guest at the bed and breakfast. During those eight days I had no responsibilities at all except to bathe, eat, sleep, study the Bible, pray, fast and listen to God.

This was an opportunity for a new beginning, and it was exactly what I needed to give me a new perspective, to say the least! God provided transportation there and back and paid the bill in full. He was proving to me that I could not out give Him!

I did some writing while I was there, too. **When someone has physical surgery, that person likes to talk about it. Well, I had big time major spiritual surgery, so I wrote about it for the glory of God.**

# BED & BREAKFAST

A Heavenly haven of rest
Is where I am today
For eight days in fact
Sure glad I did pray

God brought me here
He met me here too
Because He had
A powerful work to do

As I fasted and prayed and studied the Word
God talked to me
Gave me understanding
Helped me see what I couldn't before see

When things are seen from God's viewpoint
It makes a big difference indeed
With love and understanding came healing
No more does my heart bleed

I see clearly the damage done
By emotional abuse over the years
Jesus lifted me from the cocoon of pain
And wiped away my tears

Jesus held me in His loving arms
Spoke to my heart so gently
Letting me know I'm to raise a standard
No more abuse for me

I'm God's child and I'm special
I'm to be treated accordingly
Not because of my righteousness
But because of Christ in me

When abuse comes my way
It is Christ in me
That is being rejected
This should not be

I choose to keep my spiritual eyes open
I choose to see what God sees
I choose to use wisdom and understanding
And it is the Lord I aim to please

It will take faith, but that's okay
I hear and obey God's Word daily
He faithfully leads me step by step
What more can I say

As He has been faithful to me
So shall He receive the same from me
This way we're both very happy
To God be the glory

*"And said unto him, Go, wash in the pool of Siloam, (which is by interpre-*
*tation, Sent.) He went his way therefore, and washed, and came seeing,"*
*(John 9:7)*

**I prayed for my pathway to healing, and the Lord led me accordingly.**

# 15. TRANSFORMATION BEGINS

LITTLE DID I KNOW THE BREAKTHROUGH that had just begun. As I arrived at the Faith Acres Bed and Breakfast and toured the beautiful home filled with antiques, there was no way I could have known the surgery about to be performed ... supernaturally. God did it. I needed it. He knew it. He supplies all my needs (*Philippians 4:19*). What did He do?

As I read the Bible, fasted some, read the book about the emotionally abused woman and prayed, I began to experience a release from the bondage I had been in. Each truth God showed me exposed the darkness I had been in and broke the strong bond that was holding me captive. It was painful at the time because it was like opening a wound and having it cleansed by God's love, and then He sealed it shut and made me stronger than ever before in that area. It was a gradual process; I could not have withstood the pain had it been one instantaneous release.

The best way I can explain it is that when past experiences or incidents came to mind I invited Jesus to walk into that dark area with me and to fill it with light and truth. He did. The darkness was exposed and the enemy, satan, could no longer torment my mind about that particular scene because the darkness was gone. Jesus set me free from condemnation and fear and took away the pain of the memory as only He can. Then I rested, praised Him, and prepared for the next round.

I am not a boxer (obviously!) but I was in the ring for more than ten rounds, that I can tell you. Every blow received was relived and I was relieved of the pain, the unforgiveness, the bitterness, hatred, sorrow and fear, only to have them replaced with such peace and healing. No bruises, cuts, incisions or stitches. Surgery was done from the INSIDE. When Jesus performs surgery there are no scars. **JESUS is my MASTER SURGEON!**

As I think back it was like being in the boxing ring with Jesus and with the devil at the same time. Each time I made a decision to be healed of something from the past—for example, the wounds caused by cruel words— Jesus responded to the cry of my heart and did a quick work. When the initial memory of the experience surfaced, pain and torment surfaced too as the devil attacked viciously. The enemy of my soul did not want me to get free.

I made a quality decision though. I knew I was falling to the mat slowly and could not continue standing much longer. When words wound your spirit and fester, there is much pain. After a period of years the poison gains entrance to a much larger area than the original wound. Your whole being becomes infected, and it affects every area of your life. The devil loves it when he can subtly cause this to happen.

Arthritis can be caused by unforgiveness. The more the hurts stockpile, the greater the denial and the more severe the arthritis, asthma, etc. I have observed it in myself to a degree and in others close to me. When healing, forgiveness and love flowed once again, the physical body reflected the changes because there was no more dis...ease; no more disease. The Word of God says, "*My people are destroyed for lack of knowledge...*" (*Hosea 4:6*). Sometimes we are guilty of rejecting knowledge. There are repercussions. We need to study and learn the truth from God.

I had been in denial. I knew I hurt, but I was deceived into thinking that I had no way out of the abuse since I did not believe divorce was an option. Yes, I kept coming to the Lord for healing, but hardly a day went by that I didn't receive wounds to my spirit.

They were too painful to deal with; it was easier to go into denial, although I did not consciously decide to do so. It became my "**coping mechanism**." I was not looking at the long term results.

It's rather like when a person begins to eat more than he or she really needs. It opens a door and starts a process. The person gains five pounds the first year, then ten pounds the next year, and a little bit more year after year. The problem gets bigger and bigger each year because the problem was never dealt with when it first started.

The person just continued to bend the boundaries until the waistline needed elastic to compensate for the results. Give the enemy an inch and he will take it as far as you allow him to take it—size 6, 16, 20, and on and on. Like quicksand traps you and sucks you down and down until you are overcome, the devil keeps pulling you down and down if your flesh is weak.

# 16. BIRTHING A TIGER

Spiritually, I was like a pregnant woman about to give birth. There was no more room to stockpile any more pain. I needed to deliver. It was time. God knew it, so He provided a beautiful lavender delivery room at the Bed and Breakfast. Day ran into night and morning arrived, blending one day into the next until I felt caught up in a fog of some kind.

My mind questioned if this time away from home was a time of refreshing or a time of confusion and pain. I did not understand what was happening at first, but I knew God was in it, so I kept praying and He kept revealing more and more to me.

I was in a cocoon of deception. Each time God revealed something that set me free, I was able to face truth and come out of denial, and I emerged a little more from the cocoon. It was very gradual, but it was happening, and then it happened.

I envisioned the form of Lazarus as Jesus called him forth and the grave clothes were removed. He emerged from that tomb of death to a new life. So it was with me. I emerged from that birthing room a new woman. I had been resurrected and birthed out of that cocoon ready to write of the miracles I received—the new zeal, new joy, new freedom, new everything—because, "*If the Son therefore shall make you free, ye shall be free indeed,*" (*John 8:36*).

Little did I know that I would feel so transparent as I began to write of my experiences, but it was necessary. Jesus was transparent, His heart wide open with no secrets. He caused my tongue to be like the "*...pen of a ready writer.*" (*Psalm 45:1*).

I envisioned a horn of plenty and then saw myself emerge from that horn with both arms fully outstretched. In my left hand was a pen, and in my right hand was paper. An Author was birthed out of that cocoon of deception. God told me the title of honor he bestowed on me was "Author."

I was delighted, because it had to mean I learned something that would be helpful to others.

I returned home after eight days in that Upper Room and came home a changed woman. I instantly recognized when Clint abused me verbally, or any other way. **We are to submit to authority, not be controlled by authority. There is a big difference.**

I instantly recognized the control and manipulation he was trying to use against me. My senses were sharpened to discern immediately the abuse of authority, and my spirit man rose up against it too. Fear was knocking at the same time, but I was determined to obey the Holy Spirit and confront.

I told Clint he was not to speak to me with such disrespect. He answered that he would talk to me whatever way he wanted to. Again, I reminded him that he was to show respect to me. He did not like me speaking up. I knew by his responses that my words were angering him. Yet my help came from God, so I was determined to obey.

Each time I confronted Clint he saw me gain strength I did not have before. It angered him to see me gaining confidence. It appeared we were fighting each other, but I knew I was in a fiery spiritual battle. An unseen devil was influencing every ungodly remark and action that I faced. Each encounter was an opportunity to grow spiritual muscles as I learned how to battle in the realm of the spirit using the Word of God.

**God instructed me to do this for ten weeks!** I did not know why it was to be ten weeks specifically, but I did promise not to do anything else in that timeframe, which meant I was not to separate or file for divorce. It was not fun at all. Clint met my new attitude and strength with denial, frustration and anger, yet I stood my ground and refused to lower the standard in our home. I raised it up where it should have been raised—much higher. **Jesus has high standards and Christians should too.**

As the end of the ten-week period neared, Clint increased his attempts to manipulate and control me. As a result, I had no job, no money, no car and no friends—they would not come to see me for fear of running into my husband, nor did they phone much. Bill collectors were phoning daily, and I never knew when Clint would walk in the door. Sometimes he was gone seven days and there was no contact at all. Other times he was gone two days then showed up for twenty-four hours, totally exhausted. We planned nothing, we did nothing together, yet life continued.

I tried not to live with one foot out the door ready to leave. I tried not to start packing boxes in an effort to be prepared for what seemed like the inevitable. I tried to have the right attitude towards my husband regardless of his attitude. I tried, but I did not always succeed. God was still doing a work in me. I was thankful for His grace and forgiveness and for giving me patience, too.

Since I had begun standing against Clint's abuse, it seemed the tables turned and I saw my husband in denial. He denied abusing me and tried to excuse and justify his behavior, refusing to discuss it. In his mind he was doing nothing wrong and had no problem. He also did not want to get help because he believed he did not need any. This meant he did not have to change or to take any responsibility, let alone be accountable to anyone.

One night during this time God began doing a deeper work in my heart as I was convicted of verbally abusing Clint. I was still taking offense at his behavior and was having a hard time forgiving him. I repented and invited the Holy Spirit to teach me how to be a better wife. Instead of pointing a finger at my husband I saw fingers pointing at me. It made me want to do better.

I did not like the 'me' I saw. Instead of being in denial, now I had made a 180-degree turn. I came out of denial, took charge, and was ready to take on anyone in the whole world that tried to manipulate and control me, let alone abuse me verbally, physically, or any other way. I was like a tiger out of the cage defying anyone to DARE abuse me!! No wonder my husband withdrew. If you rock on a cat's tail, would you want to be near its head?

My husband's reaction was to deny being abusive, to lie repeatedly, to avoid confrontation, to withdraw and watch television and to virtually abandon me. As he shut down emotionally, mentally and physically, the marriage died. Clint actually agreed that the marriage had died, but rather than take any responsibility or try to resurrect it, he laid the responsibility on God. In Clint's mind, it was up to God to resurrect our marriage, not up to him to do anything about it.

It seemed to me that Clint was being too passive, not showing any responsibility or remorse or anything. Just leave it all in God's capable hands, so if it does not work, blame Him! I did not believe that way. So I sat there, typing from my heart, while trusting God to do a work that only He could do within our hearts.

I was willing to believe for a miracle and that our marriage would finally bring glory to God. That would be wonderful. But at the same time I was very aware that I was changing because I had chosen to yield to the Holy Spirit.

Whether my marriage was intact or not, I wanted to be made completely whole. I did not want to limit God. He could absolutely heal my entire being because Jesus paid the price for me to be made whole—spirit soul, and body. My marital status would not hinder me from growing when I was willing to be pliable in the Master Potter's hands. My free will was involved, and God would not violate that free will. The more I yielded to Him, the more I became like Jesus. Praise the Lord.

Meanwhile, though, *"Why sit we here until we die?"* (2 Kings 7:3). That's kind of how I viewed the situation. As far as I was concerned, each day that passed was one day closer to the return of the Lord Jesus Christ, and I wanted to produce good fruit, not simply exist, hanging around and waiting for Clint to make the next move.

**But GOD ... told me to wait ten weeks, so I was determined to wait!** *"Trust in the Lord with all your heart and lean not to your own understanding. In all your ways acknowledge him, and he will make your paths straight,"* (*Proverbs 3:5,6 NIV*). I began a countdown, and it was fifteen days ... before the ten weeks were completed.

# 17. COUNTDOWN BEGINS

I OPENED THE PATIO DOOR TO let the dog in, not realizing I had just lit a fuse. I heard Clint's voice raise in protest letting me know he did not want me to let the dog in. I looked at him and told him to stop yelling. Then I said, *"Do you realize what you are doing? You are angry because I let the dog in the house, that is all! This is ridiculous."*

I walked toward the kitchen sink and he started up again. I turned to him and yelled back saying, *"I think you need to hear how silly this is, shouting and angry because the dog came in. Now stop."* I walked toward the sink again, and he continued to complain.

As the water was running, I put my hand under the faucet and shook the water off towards him. *"Here now, cool off."* I felt a few sprinkles leave my hand and fly across the kitchen island between us as he sat at the dining room table a few feet away.

Instantly he jumped up, sucked in his breath, and when I saw his face I could see he was livid. He was instantly out of control. I started to back up as he reached for a decorative wooden rocker that sat on the kitchen island. The rocker was a few feet tall and held a plant. He lifted it and aimed it at me. I turned and ran toward the laundry room off the kitchen as fast as I could. I heard the crash and turned briefly to see if he was still coming toward me. He had stopped and started back toward the dining room. There was broken glass and hot chocolate everywhere.

It was a mess. When I saw that he was retreating to the dining room, I did an about turn and grabbed the cordless telephone because it was the only phone in the house that worked. As I started to dial 911, Clint said, *"They won't do anything."* His voice was suddenly and completely calm. He looked at the phone and I made the call. He protested again. I told him, *"I don't care, I am not waiting for you to hit me next after this behavior. At least it will be documented."*

He went from the dining room into the back bedroom, then came out and sat in his recliner. He was waiting for the law to arrive so he parked himself in his comfort zone. I went to my room and changed from shorts to slacks. When I came out, he said, *"Yeah, you better put some clothes on."* I did not respond to him. I kept the phone in my hand. I kept distance between the two of us.

It was a while before the law arrived, but I had been sure they would be there any minute, so I called the dog and opened the patio door to let him outside because he barked incessantly when anyone came to the door. As soon as I called the dog to come, Clint barged out of the den where he had gone to watch television and said, *"No, no, he is not going out."* I closed the door because the dog was already out by then.

My husband rushed toward me as I stood at the patio doors. He told me not to close the blinds or he would hurt me. He reached up and grabbed the valance that was over the patio doors and tore it to the floor, vertical blinds and all. I had no intention of closing the blinds and was not touching the cord at all. I backed away from him into the kitchen, in great fear.

The whole situation was so senseless. He had overreacted both times and was "losing it," so to speak. I stood there very afraid. It reminded me of the time Clint's son asked me if I had seen his dad throw one of his fits yet. Then he started laughing. I didn't laugh. I had just arrived in the USA and his comment put me on the alert. Little did I know then ... what I would face in the near future.

The police came and I was very relieved. We each told our side of the events, and I filled out a report. I was afraid to stay in the house after the law left, and since I did not have a car and my husband would not let me use his, the police drove me to a friend's home for the night.

I packed my suitcase in a hurry and left, giving Clint a phone number where he could leave a message if he needed to (my brother was in intensive care in the hospital in Canada after an auto accident, and I wanted to be reachable in case there was any news). But I purposely did not give the number where I would be staying that night or the address. I wanted to protect the people I stayed with.

God gives wisdom. (A little point, but very important if you are the sort of person who is kind enough to open your home to someone in need and do not want to be sought out by someone who is angry, violent, abusive, etc.)

I did not have to make a decision because my husband's actions made the decision for me. Earlier that day I had told Clint I wanted to have a relationship with him and make our marriage work (despite what seemed to be inevitable, I was still hoping for a miracle). He agreed we would try. In just a few minutes he was yelling at me and putting me down.

I reminded him that we had decided to try to work on our marriage. He said, "*Well if you stop the hell-raisin'.*" I just looked at him. He always turned things around in his mind so he would not ever have to be accountable.

In the length of time it took to drink a coffee, Clint and I sat in the living room and I tried to talk with him about our marriage. His ideas were so out of line. For example, he told me he believed it was okay for him to see someone else as long as they didn't have sex. I let him know I was not interested in sharing his divided heart, and if that is how he thought, he was already committing adultery.

He said if I divorced him I could not marry again. I looked at him and said nothing. That was the last thing I had on my mind for sure. He repeated himself. He was fishing. I looked up and said, "*If I wanted to, yeah.*" He said he would ask a couple he knew because he valued their opinion. I told him he needed to get God's opinion. People's opinions are not important. He did not like that and he left the room.

Once he was gone I began praying. I found myself praying for Clint and for some other woman, and I asked God to expose all darkness. I knew in my heart that Clint had been talking with another woman for several months, so I went to him and confronted him.

His eyes filled with tears and he kept staring at me. I did not even blink. He got so embarrassed he stood up and walked out. He left without a word and did not come back until late that night. He really thought I did not know.

**I know ... what GOD ... wants me to know! I trusted God to reveal truth. I prayed God would not let Clint touch me if he was seeing another woman. He ceased touching me sexually.** God knows everything. He was fighting this battle, not me. I was standing in faith with peace in my heart. I knew that all this persecution I was going through would result in heavenly rewards, and that I would have all of eternity to enjoy those precious rewards. As for the suffering, I was in good company. Jesus was right with me 24/7 (still is!) and He suffered far more than I ever will. Praise His Name.

After praying, I phoned the couple Clint had gone to see. The wife answered and I said, "*Since my husband values your opinion a lot, I want you to know something. He told me this afternoon that he is seeing someone, and he says as long as they don't have sex it is okay. Yet I am at home waiting for my husband to come home. I would like to know what your opinion is of that since I doubt that he is telling you what he told me.*"

She was speechless. I waited. She could not speak. I waited some more. Then I said, "*It is okay, why don't you just discuss it with him.*" God had shown me he was at their home. He reveals things by the Holy Ghost. It is not spooky. It was God working on my behalf. **It was wonderful not having to look over my shoulder, having a clear conscience, being able to walk with my chin up and make the best of every situation with God's help. Honesty and integrity pay good dividends. Glory to God.**

"*... The righteous are bold as a lion,*" (*Proverbs 28:1*). That is the Word of God too. Before I was saved I was very introverted, but not anymore.

When Clint got home he told me he and his friends had a good laugh over my phone call. I said, *"God does not laugh at sin!"* God confirmed he had gone there. It is so cool when God gives the upper edge. He reveals the strategy of the enemy.

He reveals things in visions too. In the next chapter, I will share a vision that He gave me four years earlier, the full meaning of which was still being revealed to me bit by bit.

# 18. VIVID VISION

We were at church, and during the service I went to the altar for prayer. The power of God touched me and the next moment I was like a feather, lying on the floor. This is what I saw immediately thereafter. I was swimming in very deep water, using my left arm to stroke through the water. My right arm was curled around my husband's neck in an effort to rescue him. He was conscious but not making any effort to swim. For some reason he was just there, and I was trying to get to shore.

Every now and then both of us would go under the water. I saw the water with my eyes open, and it was clear. I saw bubbles, but then we came to the top again. This kept happening again and again as I was not strong enough to pull both of us to safety. There were no boats or anything at all around us—nothing in sight at all; no airplanes, nothing. No land, just very deep water but I kept swimming. It was a fight to survive.

Suddenly I felt something hit my shin and it frightened me. I thought it might be a shark and wondered if there were any in the area. I tried to look but couldn't see anything. Then it happened again—something hit my leg, but I did not know what it was. I felt my knee hit, and as my right arm released my husband I realized my legs were hitting the bottom. I had reached bottom. There was land. There was a sandy beach. It was incredible.

Gasping for breath and trying to stand up I saw people as I looked ahead and to the left. The people were on the beach looking at the water and at things other people were selling. I wondered why they made no effort to help us. Then I realized they could not see me. I could see them, but they were totally oblivious to the fact that I was there. My next thought was, *"Am I dead?!!"*

I stood up and turned to my right to see how my husband was doing. He was not next to me. I quickly looked down at the water, thinking he was still down there, but he was gone. I looked up again, and just to my right I saw Jesus in a white robe walking away from me. He had my husband in His arms, carrying him like a baby.

There was only one set of footprints in the sand. I stood there and knew Clint would be okay because he was with Jesus, and I knew Jesus would not turn around to see if I was okay because He knew I was. Then the vision stopped and I got up off the floor at the church.

Since then, as I have sought the Lord in prayer, He has given me understanding of the dream. I believe He showed me that I was interceding for my husband and trying to walk in love and be a good wife, yet Clint would not get motivated spiritually. He would not even try. This was symbolized by his not trying to swim. It hindered me a great deal because I had to carry him. He was content to be like a baby with a pacifier. Not me. However, it was too much for me and that is why every now and then we both went under the water. God brought us back up for more air until we reached shore.

I hit bottom, then landed. Then a word was given at church about women being abused by their husbands. I went to the altar. I knew that this was when I reached the shoreline. This was a turning point; this was when I let go of what was attempting to drown me. I no longer swam. I began to walk again unhindered as Jesus carried my husband away.

At first I thought the vision meant Clint was going to die. Then I realized if he died, Jesus would not be carrying him anywhere. He'd be absent from the body and be in Heaven ... or in Hell. I did know for sure that I felt very relieved ... not to have to carry him anymore. A huge burden lifted. *"Therefore we are always confident, knowing that, whilst we are at home in the body, we are absent from the Lord,"* (2 Corinthians 5:6).

In my vision I heard my name called as I stood on that beach. I looked up and Jesus was nowhere among the people. He called me again. I said, *"Where are You?"* He said, *"Turn around."* I did, and sure enough there He was, in all His splendor, standing on the water away from the shoreline with hands outstretched to me as He simply said, "*COME.*"

Once again I had it 'backwards.' I was looking in one direction and He was in the opposite direction. All the more meaningful to me, and God knew this. He doesn't overlook anything.

My first thought was of fear. Facing all that water, knowing I did not swim, was not helping me find peace within. **I had to change my focus, and when I looked into the eyes of Jesus, love beckoned me—love that made me want to step onto that water and keep right on walking. That is exactly what I did. I had come too far to turn back now.**

We embraced; He swung me around in circles, took my hand, and we continued walking together with no fear. Joy had taken over. It partnered with love, and if ever the entire world seemed completely removed, it was in that moment. Ecstasy is an understatement. No one thrills the heart like Jesus. I was shown all of this in the very short time I lay on the altar. I opened my eyes and stood up knowing my life was fixin' to change big time. That was just fine by me. I just did not know how soon.

# 19. LEGAL MISHMASH

So now, approximately four years after that vision, we put the house up for sale. I knew Clint really wanted to keep the five acres and get rid of the mobile home, but I was still in it and stood my ground. The house did not sell, so I suggested lowering the price. He refused. I suggested renting it to his son and he hung up on me. I guess that hit a nerve. The truth always surfaces. A little boy we knew innocently said that he, his mom and Clint's son were all going to live in the house—my house! This was proof that Clint had no intention of selling the house. He just wanted me out. The child's mother was completely embarrassed when she realized her son had let me know what was going on.

I told them all, though, not to be embarrassed by what this child said because it was simply the fulfillment of God's Word: *"For there is nothing hid, which shall not be manifested: neither was anything kept secret, but that it should come abroad,"* (Mark 4:22). I had perfect peace, but Clint sure didn't. The enemy does not like his plan to be found out. Serving God has benefits, such as not being in the dark when an ambush is set up or a lie is told. There is no darkness in the Lord. God's strategies always supersede those of the enemy. I choose to stay on God's side ... FOREVER!!!

I kept praying and seeking the Lord for direction. It was stressful. Often when we most need to hear that "still, small voice" within (*1 Kings 19:12*), it seems it is the most silent. The Lord did lead me though. Peace in my heart was my umpire (*Colossians 3:15*).

Before Clint and I were separated, when we discussed the material things, he said I had to pay the credit cards. We bought a washer and dryer for the house and he sent me to pick it out so it was in my name. When we bought a new sectional sofa, he and I shopped together and went home without purchasing one. Half an hour after returning home he decided which one he wanted and sent me to buy it with a credit card I had to apply for in—you guessed it—my name. He refused to go back to the store with me. Now he was saying I could have the furniture, but that was all. He did not want me to get any of his pension, yet we were married over ten years so I was legally entitled to part of it.

In my heart I didn't care about the material things because I knew God was my Source and He could do a lot better for me than part of someone's pension. **I heard one thing from God.** *"Don't fight."* **He also said,** *"Light does not leave."* I had no unction to start packing. I had no money for storage buildings or for a truck to ship my things to Canada. I did not know how long the electricity would be connected, and since the house had not sold, Clint cancelled a two-month mortgage check and tried to fast forward the house into foreclosure. That could happen within twenty-four days.

Living in the country with no car and all of the above circumstances meant I could have felt like a sitting duck—totally vulnerable—yet that is not how I felt at all. I might add that we lived in what is called "Tornado Alley," with no basement under the house.

Realizing I was very tired and did not have the strength to move anyway, I made a decision to make the best of the situation. I was going to rest, get built up spiritually and renew my mind more because that is where the battle originates—in the mind. I was going to stand my ground, keep the faith, relax and read a good book—the Bible.

I was so aware of the fact that I was just passing through on this earth. Heaven is my Hometown. It was important to me to make each day count for the Lord, even in the midst of such a mess. My phone was not ringing off the hook with people who had prayed through and had a word of knowledge or prophecy, or great words of encouragement for me.

The mortgage company phoned to apply as much pressure as possible. I hung up on them a few times and learned to bite my tongue. One day I told them what they did NOT want to hear, that my husband did not want the mobile home. In fact, he wanted them to take it away. That really rattled their chains. So they kept phoning. I think they thought if there was no answer it might mean someone had towed the house away. Then they would really be out of pocket. God helped me endure, and I know I gained a lot of patience. It was a learning experience. I rebuked fear in Jesus' Name and answered the phone. I chose to make my phone serve me, rather than me serving it out of fear.

The devil put a stranglehold on my finances, but God helped me to enjoy the beautiful surroundings and central air as I trusted Him to bring me through the fiery furnace. **It became a fiery furnace with central air! Cool or what?**

There were times I thought about a testimony I had once heard and wondered if one day I might also find a live chicken in the yard for dinner. It would have taken a miracle for me to cut its head off though. Thankfully it did not come to that.

I did apply to legal aid to inquire about getting a protective order. A friend provided me with transportation. I learned that the police officer's report of the last time they came to our home said it appeared my husband shoved the decorative rocker off the counter, so it did not prove he threw it at me. It did not hit me, nor did he strike me. In plain language, tough bananas! It seemed I had to get beat up, then I could press charges. I felt betrayed by the law.

I can adamantly tell you that when one is manipulated and controlled and frightened to the degree I was, there is much damage to the spirit man. We are not just a physical body. We are a three-part being: spirit, soul and body. The wounds to my spirit and soul were far more damaging than anything ever done to my body. Yet this was an aspect that was not considered serious as far as the law was concerned.

Think of a time when uplifting words were spoken to you. How did you feel? What was their effect on you? Now do the same with damaging words. The feelings are very real. You either receive love or a fiery dart that wounds your spirit man. *"Death and life are in the power of the tongue; and they that love it shall eat the fruit thereof,"* (Proverbs 18:21). That is truth!

Since I understood how the law worked with regard to a restraining order, I chose to continue to pray and trust God to protect me. He had done a good job to that point, and since He doesn't change *(Malachi 3:6)* I expected Him to continue. Being in the world, but not of it *(John 8:23)*, meant I did not do things the same as the world did. I was not under the world's system. I knew that the Kingdom of God was in me. With Jesus at the helm, I would get through successfully.

# 20. REALITY

I had forgotten
What it was like
To go to someone's home
And be shown unconditional love
To be received with open arms
Just as I am
No rejection
No putdowns
No abuse
No walls
No barriers
No bashing at all
Just
Plain
Love
And
Acceptance

It was like oil
Soothing my soul
As I sat in peace
Observing people
Relating with each other
Without yelling, arguing
Without being abusive

They were just having fun
It was family
Being family
The way a family
Is supposed to be
And they
Included me
It is that simple
That profound
But not a coincidence
Most definitely
It was God
Loving
Me
Reminding me
What a family is like
Should be like
Can be like
And what a family
Can do to help someone
Whose heart is broken
Whose mind feels warped
Because of years of abuse
Whose dreams have been shattered
Whose hopes have been crushed
Because one wonders if the future
Will ever be bright at all

Yet, somehow
While watching children play
In the living-room

The dog included as well
Hearing laughter ring out
Along with squeals of delight
As the dog is chased around a coffee table
Something happens deep within
Because reality is seen

Reality being
This is what it is all about
Being together
Being real
Letting love flow freely
From hearts that Jesus holds from within

It cannot happen
When a heart is deceitful
The sinful heart must hide sin within walls
The walls hold the person in sin
A prisoner to their own behavior
Bound by their decisions in life
That do not line up with the Bible

It is not complicated at all
It is called yielding to the sinful nature
But it does not have to be that way
God gave everyone a free will
He will not force people to do right

So what does one do
When learning the price to be paid
For sin

Is death
Because the wages of sin is death *(Romans 6:23)*
That's the Word of God
So I know it is true

I know what I did
I chose life
That is why my walls are down
My heart is open
My trust is in God
I am standing on the Word
Believing for grace, wisdom, understanding
And I know that it is going to be okay
Because as long as I keep my heart right
God will see me through

Decisions others have made
Are decisions others will have to answer for
My heart is open
Cleansed, purified
And in the vine
I choose to abide *(John 15:4-5)*
Jesus is the answer
He is with me I know
And will be with me
Wherever I go

He may put the solitary in families *(Psalms 68:6),*
He may bring folks to me
But whatever He does

I know I will
Be happy

Jesus saves, heals, delivers
Jesus restores
Jesus loves me
I'm so glad to be part
Of his family
The Family of God
That's
REALITY

# 21. SHHHHHHHH...BE STILL

My fingernails are only so long
Biting them at this rate
Is not accomplishing anything good
But the flames in this furnace are so hot
I can barely see
Let alone think straight

I plunged myself prostrate on the carpet
Baring my soul before God
Because He knows how I feel anyway
I said, *"I don't want to live like this anymore!"*
The tears fell; I wailed in pain, agony, and grief
Yet there was no relief

When God says, *"Be still…"* *(Psalms 46:10)*, I had better be still
So that is what I have been doing for one month now
The more still I am, the more still He is
Yet I know He is with me
The deeper the stillness
The closer we become

The greater the storm
The greater the need to persevere
The end result is in God's hands
I just need to stand in faith
I can't please God without it *(Hebrews 11:6)*
So I will stand and hold my peace

My hope is in the Lord, not man
My trust is in the Lord and His Word
He does not let anyone down
He does not break promises
It may look like all hell has broken loose
But I know differently because God's patience
Wears out the devil

God knows how to turn the tables very well
Everyone will reap what he/she sows (*Galatians 6:7*)
Someone abandoned me, cheated on me, lied to me
Dishonored me, betrayed me, abused me repeatedly
Because that someone was a backslider, denying Jesus
Living a double-life repeatedly

I choose to forgive and move forward with Jesus
I choose to stand on God's Word
Knowing He will restore
How, who, where, when
I don't know, but I do know God will restore
And more

Praise the Lord
I do not have to fight the battle
Jesus did it at Calvary
As I hold my peace, stay focused, persevere
Walk by faith too
God will see me through

Glory to God

# 22. SURROGATE GRANDMA

Someone knocked on the front door
It was a nine-year-old neighbor
She saw my little dog
In the backyard alone
Went out to play with him
Since I was on the phone

Soon I heard voices
Like music to my ears through the open window
I discovered a second young lady
On the opposite side of the fence
Chatting cheerfully to the first
It was a moment for which my soul did thirst

After greeting this twelve-year-old girl
I discovered she was a new neighbor next door
I invited her to come inside the fenced yard
To play ball and meet my dog too
She accepted the invitation and I smiled
Knowing this is what she wanted to do

Soon the girls were laughing
The dog barked and chased the ball
I sat on a lawn chair and observed
Whilst yet another visitor came
This five-year-old young man was not about to be excluded
He joined his sister and her friend knowing he had not intruded

His left brain instincts showed up immediately
He focused on the dog more than on the girls
As I observed the backyard activities
It was like removing a pause button
On a video tape
From perfect stillness and lack of life to action, and I could relate

This is what a backyard is for
People to enjoy and have fun
Mind you, the birds stopped parking on the fence posts
But I did not mind at all
Joy filled my heart as others were having fun
I knew it was something God had done
You see, God knows I've been home
With no job and no car
For over a month now
He provided transportation to church Wednesday and Sunday
He also provided children whose Grandma was away
I knew it was not a coincidence that these visitors came to play

People need people and God knows who to send
I made myself available to Him and WOW
When we went inside we talked about Jesus
All three children smiled from ear to ear
The glory of God filled the kitchen
We knew He was near

The conversation about music
Proved to provide an unexpected blessing
One young lady stood up

And a solo, acapella
She began to sing
I said silently … *"God, You can do anything!"*

When there came another knock on the door
It was more of the new neighbors
Looking for the young singer
She skipped out the door happily
As I waved at her mom who was by the fence
She knew all was well, smiled and waved back at me

I sat down to reflect for a bit
Because new memories had just been made
It was important to savor them
To appreciate what God had just done
My home received a breakthrough indeed
No more does my heart bleed

In fact, I had forgotten that
A cookie could be eaten
So many different ways
Until I observed these three young'uns
It sure is great being a "Surrogate Grandma" for a while
And even greater to obey God, be still, and watch the memories stockpile

# 23. DARKNESS FLEES

GOD TOLD ME THAT DARKNESS, NOT light, must leave. The next day Clint called and told me he was not coming home anymore. He would just come in one day the next week to get his things. He said that he was moving out and washing his hands of everything. He did not want a divorce, but he did want me out of the country.

He did not know God told me not to do anything until after ten weeks had passed. Clint's manipulation was not working, because I stayed even though my job and car and money were gone and he had cancelled two months' mortgage payments on the house. **Apparently he did hear me say that I could not change him, but with God's help I could change me.**

There is only one way the enemy can get to someone—through deception. For example, if a man says he is not abusive, pointing to the fact that he has never been arrested as evidence, it by no means proves he is not abusive. It just means that he has never been arrested for abuse! In my husband's case, he had not yet been found guilty by the law. There are a lot of people doing bad things that they have not yet been arrested for doing, but the lack of arrest does not prove them innocent.

My consolation was the fact that each time I called 911 they had a record of the incident. That documentation could be used in court to help the next woman my husband might abuse. Clint denied needing help. **Abusers follow a pattern. Abuse is transferred from one victim to another until the cycle is stopped.**

I became more aware of this as I packed up his things before he came to pick them up. As I was packing, I found a note I had written some time before. It was a list of five things my spouse could do to make our marriage work. I have to admit, I did not think it was asking too much since it was coming from his wife.

The list read:

1. Speak to me with respect.
2. Look at me when you talk to me.
3. Be cleaned up by 7 p.m. one or two nights a week and look forward to spending an evening together, but not always at home.
4. Dine with me and sleep with me, pray and read the Word with me.
5. Be the Priest of our home.

Sadly, these things did not transpire, so here I was packing up his belongings.

I felt nervous knowing he would be coming to the house. I prayed for peace and grace and to not fear man. My senses sharpened each time a vehicle passed down the road, and it made me aware of how much it affected me. Fear was coming against me. My nerves were on edge. It was like driving a car when you know the tire has a slow leak. Not a good feeling, whether you are in the fast lane or the Grannie lane.

It made me realize how much I had to walk on eggs, so to speak, when he was around. My purpose was to avoid making him angry, but it did not work. I was giving in to the fear and manipulation so the problem was not solved. I enabled it to grow.

**The best thing I ever did was expose the abuse over and over again for those ten weeks. The more I did, the more I became aware of how much abuse there was. It brought me more and more out of denial, whether Clint wanted to deal with the abuse or not.** I was like the coal oil lantern whose shade was being cleaned of all soot. I could see the truth in a much different light. It was so clear to me now. Then it appalled me that I had lived that way for so long, but better late than never to put an end to it.

I was actually prepared for this day because we had lived like a divorced couple for several months—years, actually—sleeping in separate rooms, growing apart in all other areas as well. Yet when he came to the house for his stuff, he continued to say he did not want a divorce. I was no longer in denial and I did want a divorce. Given my circumstances, who wouldn't?

I thought about the vision the Lord had given me of Clint and me in the water, approaching the shore. I recalled that as Jesus carried him away across the sandy beach, they did not ascend. Jesus was walking on the sand, so he was carrying my husband somewhere, but away from me. Spiritual death is different from physical death. I believe Clint had suffered spiritual death because of sin, hardening his heart, rebellion, not going to church, holding back tithes, betraying me, not coming home, abandonment, unfaithfulness, etc. The Bible does say liars have no place in the kingdom of God (*Revelation 21:8*).

I prayed for Clint specifically because of the stronghold of lying that had hold of him. It was clear that Clint had become desensitized to the Holy Spirit as he continued to do his own thing, go his own way. When you keep shutting someone out, there comes a time when you do not hear their voice at all. When a husband treats his wife the way Clint treated me, God will not hear his prayers. Of course, the same is true of wives if they mistreat their husbands.

More than once my husband would go into another room and pray for an hour then emerge from the room downcast and shaking his head saying, "*Nothing.*" He heard nothing. This is why. Not because I say so, it is the Word of God. It was written in the Bible for a reason. God's voice will not be heard because the person is in rebellion and has walked too far away: "*If I regard iniquity in my heart, the Lord will not hear me,*" (*Psalm 66:18*). **Everyone has a free will; God will not force anyone to obey. Nor will He wink at sin.**

At least I am glad about the fact that in the vision I had, Jesus carried him away as I stood in ankle-deep water observing, confident that Jesus knew I would be okay. What was going to happen beyond that, I didn't know. I just knew the Lord had a plan for my life. He knew all this was going to happen. *Romans 8:28* was going to apply, so I had an expectancy for something good to come out of all of this. I did not develop those spiritual muscles for nothing. I had worked hard for them by exercising my faith as I worked the Word, believed the Word, and proclaimed the Word over the years.

So I stayed positive even when Clint refused to apply himself spiritually. He did not want to pray and take spiritual authority as the Priest of our home. As a result, he was like a baby with a pacifier who refuses to mature spiritually. Yet his lack of applying himself spiritually did not stop me from doing so. I became stronger and knew that whatever was next, those muscles were not developed in vain. They would be used. Things have a way of dovetailing in the spirit realm. There is always a higher mountain to climb, so my efforts were not in vain. In fact, nothing I do in an effort to please God is ever in vain, thankfully. The following poem is fruit of God's faithfulness to me.

# 24. PRAISE THE LORD!

The phone rang, the enemy was mad
I heard such anger and rudeness
Then fear said, *"No more home for you*
*Foreclosure, as well as a divorce, no job, no car."*
It was such a mess

Yet my security system is in the Kingdom of God
I've planted lots of seed in fertile soil for years
I trust God to send my harvest, even more than I need
So I'll not sit and fret, or be in tears

I chose to make Jesus Lord of my life
Twenty-two years ago
Not compromise the Gospel of Jesus Christ
As God does well know

So in advance, in faith
I say, Praise the Lord forevermore
To God be the Glory
For opening the door

The door where I am to go
Providing the car I need too
Not to mention the family
Because I already prayed through

In my distress I prayed to the Lord
He answered me and rescued me
He is for me
How can I be afraid
"*What can mere man do to me?*" (Psalm 118:6)
The Lord is on my side
He will help me
Let those who hate me beware

After writing this poem I read

"*I called on the Lord in distress;
The Lord answered me and set me in a broad place.
The Lord is on my side; I will not fear.
What can man do to me?
The Lord is for me among those who help me.
Therefore I shall see my desire on those who hate me.
It is better to trust in the Lord
Than to put confidence in man.*" (Psalm 118:5-8 NKJ)

"*I know your works. See, I have set before you an open door and no one can shut it; for you have a little strength, have kept My word, and have not denied My name.*" (Revelation 3:8 NKJV)

# 25. WHAT ARE YOU GOING TO DO?

THE PHONE RANG AND CLINT ASKED, *"What are you going to do?"* I answered, *"I am waiting for you to come and pick up your personal things like you said you would this week."* Then I turned it back on him and asked, "What are you going to do?" He replied, *"Well I guess I will have to move out then."* Because I was accustomed to his verbal manipulation, I tried to clarify and asked, *"Did you tell me you would come one day this week and get your personal things because you are not living here anymore, you are moving out, and you will not be back?"*

His answer was, **"Well, you won't ever call the law on me again!"** Didn't exactly answer my question. I replied, *"You hear me … you will not use manipulation and control and fear against me."* His response was to ask again, *"What are you going to do?"*

It didn't take long for me to see he just wanted to argue. Our conversations were often this bizarre. I tried to stick to the point. I knew he wanted me out of the house so he could sell or rent it, but God told me to stay. So, I told Clint that he was not my source, God was and God wouldn't let me starve because my husband wouldn't buy groceries for me. I said, **"God is going to show you that you are not in control, He is."** He had no response to that powerful statement. In fact, he stopped talking altogether. It was one of those moments when you just know the fear of the Lord is at hand.

I knew that God had just given me a word of knowledge for Clint, and I was as surprised when I said it as he was to hear it. In fact, it answered a big question for me. Now I knew why I had to stay and sit tight for so long. God does not ask anyone to do something without a purpose. Now I knew His purpose.

I told Clint, *"You may think you are putting me under a lot of stress by abandoning me and not providing food or paying bills, but let me tell you, God is looking after me. I have peace, I am enjoying my home, and I even have joy in the midst of it all because God is my Source and I know it. That's pretty good fruit."* There was no response.

He asked how the dog was and I did not answer. Instead I said, *"You might ask how your wife is because you have not looked after her."* He asked, *"Does Dan have enough food?"* I said, *"You might ask if I have enough food since you did not provide any or give any money to me. I do not have any money."* He said, "Well I guess you aren't going to tell me anything about Dan."

When I told him he would have to answer to God for abandoning me like he had, he simply said, *"Whatever."* Then I told him about a foreclosure notice I had received in the mail concerning the land. He said he did not want the land or the house. He was washing his hands of it all.

I told him he was not being responsible, had lost track of time, and that I might not be there when he got back from work that week. If the phone and electric were cut off I would have to move out with Dan and he would not know where we were living. He shouted, *"Where are you taking Dan? You better not take that dog anywhere."* I said, *"I am not going to argue with you. Bye."*

I sat down and tried to get a clear picture of what was actually happening. What was he thinking? He had called to see what I was going to do. He really wanted to know if I had filed for a divorce two weeks earlier, and if so, on what grounds I had filed. He knew it would take two weeks to get a court appointment, and the two weeks were up. He wanted to know what was going on.

With this call he tipped his hand. He was very scared that I had charged him with adultery and couldn't wait to find out what I had done and if I had named a third party. When you play, you pay, and he surely had no peace. I did not tell him anything, so he did not find out anything. He would have to sweat it out some more. That was not my doing. The fear and torment he was experiencing were the result of his choices.

You know, I felt like a grape that had been squeezed until there was little life left, but I was not giving up. I did NOT file for a divorce; I filed for social assistance. I was forced to. I received an application from welfare. A friend drove me to the office where it took two hours to fill out the paperwork. I was fingerprinted and photographed. It was humiliating, but I decided to resist shame because I was not in this situation as a result of any of my decisions. Well, some of the decisions were mine—I had enabled the abuse to continue—but that was over. I received my Lone Star card which enabled me to receive $120 worth of groceries per month for a three-month period. Suddenly, catsup, pickles and paper towels became luxury items. The Bible challenged me to learn to be content whether I had a lot or a little, (*Philippians 4:11-12*). A lot is better, but I was learning and trying to be appreciative of everything. It is amazing how few groceries one can survive on when it is necessary.

I was grieved that this had gone on for four months after my husband took my name off our bank accounts and made me beg for any money from welfare and from him. Plus, he had not made the land payments for five months at that point. He wanted me out. He did not want to pay with me living there, but he wanted the land (even though he had told me he didn't— more manipulation) so he had to pay to keep it. He couldn't rent it out either with me still living there. No wonder he was so angry. It made me wonder if he realized that he was not in control and that God was!

Clint said he did not want a divorce. My response was to ask him what he was doing to demonstrate that he did not want a divorce and that he wanted to be married. Then I thanked the Holy Spirit for those words.

He had no response. He wanted me to file. That is why he told me about a woman he was seeing, not knowing that I already knew about her. Then he said it was okay as long as they weren't having sex. So now he had to decide which scenario was worse: for him to file, or to risk my naming a third party. The woman he was involved with must have had some influence as well. While I waited to see what he would do, I listened to the Lord and obeyed. The only filing I did was for welfare assistance.

The pressure was pretty intense because I had to go out and did not know when he would come to get his personal things. It was not a good feeling when I left the house, wondering what I would find when I returned home. He had broken and destroyed things before, including tearing up our wedding photos, so what would be next? I tried to resist fear and trust God. It was a horrible situation and I would never wish it on anyone.

Another thought that came to me was that if I filed for a divorce he would file bankruptcy as he had threatened. His credit was shot anyway. He was afraid he would have to pay me, and he would rather file bankruptcy. What I did know was that the pressure he put me under would come back on him some day, through someone else, because it is the Bible principle of sowing and reaping (*Galatians 6:7*).

I knew how hard it was for me, even though I did my best to lean on the Lord, so I would not have wanted to be in his shoes. All I can say is that when people dish it out, they had better be ready to receive the same at some point because it will happen. God is just. **God is love and He is just!**

I started praising the Lord because it always helped. The teaching at church helped me get caught up in the secret place, and my home became like a prison that had miraculously had the doors flung open wide with the fresh, sweet air pouring in. The Bible talks about Paul and Silas being caught up in the glory and the presence of the Lord as they praised Him while they were in chains in prison. They did not even walk out the door as soon as it was opened, nor did anyone else (*Acts 16:22-37*). The secret place with God is the best place—a taste of heaven on earth.

I guess you can tell that I was on an emotional roller coaster, but at least my heart was still soft. **My heart was not hard, but it did hurt, and it hurt a lot.**

# 26. IT HURTS TOO MUCH

SOFT, WARM TEARS WERE FALLING AS I tried to read the Word, pray, and just bask in the presence of the Lord. He was doing a deep work in my heart and it was wonderful, yet at the same time it hurt. I didn't understand it all, but I knew it was the work of the Lord so I welcomed it, no matter how painful.

The phone rang earlier that day and it was the mortgage company, even though I had written a letter telling them not to phone any more. They wanted to know why I stopped payment on a check for two months' payment. I said, "*I didn't.*" I told them not to phone again since they had a letter and they needed to speak with my husband who no longer lived there. He was the one who had stopped the payment. I gave them the phone number for his workplace, but they became pretty forceful so I hung up. They called several more times.

I kept my peace, but it was not easy. It hurt knowing my husband had the money in the bank but would not pay in an attempt to force me to move out. It was manipulation, and it was awful. I got nasty phone calls almost every day after that, as the mortgage company was livid!

They used fear and manipulation as well, so I got lots of practice exercising my spiritual muscles—kind of like "Christian sandpaper" being used to refine. At the rate it was going, I figured I would be polished properly in no time flat. The fire was very, very hot. Thank God I knew I was not in it alone. Jesus was in the fire too!

If by chance you do not read the Bible, the fiery furnace experiences I share, also tie in with a Bible story from the book of Daniel, chapter three. The significance of the story is great, so I will give a brief account of it. King Nebuchadnezzar made an image of gold and instructed everyone to bow down and worship the gold image when the trumpet sounded.

Anyone who would not do so would be cast into the midst of a burning fiery furnace.

There were three Jews the King had set over the affairs of the province of Babylon. Their names were Shadrach, Meshach, and Abednego. They refused to bow down and worship the gold image. They claimed their God, whom they served, would deliver them from the fiery furnace and out of the King's hand.

The King heated the furnace seven times hotter, bound the three men, and threw them in. Then he looked and saw four men, not three, walking unbound in the midst of the fiery furnace. In *Daniel 3:25* the King said, "... *and they have no hurt and the form of the fourth is like the Son of God.*" The King called the three men out of the furnace.

The Bible states in *Daniel 3:27*, "*And the princes, governors, and captains, and the king's counselors, being gathered together, saw these men, upon whose bodies the fire had no power, nor was an hair of their head singed, neither were their coats changed, nor the smell of fire had passed on them.*"

*Daniel 3:28*, "*Then Nebuchadnezzar spake, and said, 'Blessed be the God of Shadrach, Meshach, and Abednego, who hath sent his angel, and delivered his servants that trusted in him, and have changed the king's word, and yielded their bodies, that they might not serve nor worship any gods except their own God.'*"

*Daniel 3:29-30*, "' *Therefore I make a decree, That every people, nation, and language, which speak any thing amiss against the God of Shadrach, Meshach, and Abednego, shall be cut in pieces, and their houses shall be made a dunghill: because there is no other God that can deliver after this sort.' Then the king promoted Shadrach, Meshach, and Abednego, in the province of Babylon.*"

**I finally refused to bow to abuse any more; I refused to bow to manipulation and control (which is witchcraft); and I refused to bow to the spirit of fear.** When I came out of denial and took a stand against abusive behavior, I raised the bar for righteousness' sake and entered the fiery furnace, so to speak. But I did not enter the furnace alone. Time and again, Jesus revealed himself to me. I was never alone. My trust in God and obedience to His voice, kept me alive and brought me out more refined and free, free, free indeed!

But back to the furnace of phone calls from irate people…the mortgage company was very upset. I was asked, *"Why are you living there?"* I kept my peace and almost snickered when I hung up because I remembered it was God who had provided thus far, and I was standing on the Word that says, *"… behold, I have set before thee an open door, and no man can shut it,"* *(Revelation 3:8)*.

I knew I would be there as long as God wanted me there. That I DID know! It would not be one day sooner and not one day later. It was fine with me. I did pray that powerful prayer, *"Thy will be done,"* *(Matthew 26:42)*. God had a purpose. He was showing my husband who was in control, and it wasn't man or woman!

I did tell God that if He wanted me to move I was willing. It did not matter that it looked like my husband was going to have his cake and eat it too; that he could abuse me, abandon me, keep the land, force foreclosure on the house and car, ruin our credit and be unfaithful, yet keep the one thing he wanted, which was the land.

What really mattered was that I was keeping my heart right with God. Above all, that was what was most important. I forgave others and kept in mind that vengeance belonged to God *(Romans 12:19-21)*, so He would deal with them because I stepped out of God's way when I let go and put my trust in God.

There are many times in the Bible when it looked like Jesus was the underdog, the loser, but Jesus was and is the ultimate winner! He never lost a battle; He won every battle and He won the war. Jesus *gave* His life; it was not taken, so even in death He won, not to mention His resurrection afterwards!

That was why, in the midst of my circumstances, I could sing and praise the Lord, have peace in my heart and actually enjoy each day because I stayed in the presence of the Lord Jesus Christ. He paid the price for me to be more than a conqueror. *Romans 8:37* says, *"Nay, in all these things we are more than conquerors through him that loved us.* I was no longer a victim; I was more than a conqueror—a survivor of abuse, attempted murder, divorce, jealousy, bullying, manipulation, control, lying, deception, and more.

I turned them all into stepping stones and moved on with the Lord. I chose to follow Jesus. I chose to obey. I chose to stand on the Word of the Lord and not fear man. I chose to soar like an eagle to new heights, above the storm, knowing God was always with me and would always see me through. No dungeon could hold me; I knew I was FREE ... in Jesus' Name. Amen.

*"He giveth power to the faint: and to them that have no might he increaseth strength. Even the youths shall faint and be weary, and the young men shall utterly fall: But they that wait upon the Lord shall renew their strength; they shall mount up with wings as eagles: they shall run and not be weary: and they shall walk and not faint,"* (Isaiah 40:29-31)

**You know, as I look back I can see the Lord's hand everywhere. He makes beauty out of ashes.** *Isaiah 61:3* says, *"To appoint unto them that mourn in Zion, to give unto them beauty for ashes, the oil of joy for mourning, the garment of praise for the spirit of heaviness; that they might be called trees of righteousness, the planting of the Lord, that he might be glorified."*

God did that bit by bit, day by day, with my life. It was being transformed by the refiner's fire daily. *"But who may abide the day of his coming? And who shall stand when he appeareth? for he is like a refiner's fire, and like fullers' soap: And he shall sit as a refiner and purifier of silver: and he shall purify the sons of Levi, and purge them as gold and silver, that they may offer unto the LORD an offering in righteousness,"* (Malachi 3:2-3).

As impurities surface when gold is heated, the same happened to me. God was purging and refining. I made the decision to stay in the furnace and trust God to help me through. Prior to complete restoration, the dross must be removed. The dross is ugly as is divorce—broken covenant with God and with man—yet divorce is a provision.

**The less deceived I became, the more I came out of denial. The more I came out of denial, the more clearly I heard from God. It also became much easier to encourage myself in the Lord.**

The more I looked up and leaned on and drew my help and peace from the Lord, the more I received. Discouragement was replaced with encouragement; fear was replaced with faith; defeat was replaced with hope. It was and is a process that occurred daily with each decision I made. **I was climbing an invisible spiritual mountain, but not in my own strength.**

Jesus gave me that tenacity. He led me every step of the way. I got to know Him a lot better and appreciated Him more in those trying years than I had in the previous twenty-two or twenty-three years; I recognized on a daily basis that He was and is there all the time. No phone or fax or computer needed, just an open heart reaching out in faith.

**Some of our sweetest, deepest moments of intimacy happened when neither of us spoke.** Love flowed freely from His heart to mine and mine to His. My eyes would fill with tears; when God's love is manifested so powerfully, no words are needed. I knew I was loved, and it was a two-way street. Without a doubt, many good things were happening regardless of my circumstances.

Daily battles were being won in the spirit realm.

Next Clint cancelled my medical insurance, which I discovered when I had to fill a prescription. It was yet another opportunity to get offended. At least I was relieved of the fear and anger. I was already sleeping a lot more soundly. It was wonderful to awaken refreshed. That was the way it should be.

Yet, it hurt to realize how much pressure I was under from manipulation and control. I had been blinded to it until ten weeks earlier. I tried not to feel ashamed or have regrets. I had to press on and praise God for setting me free and opening my eyes to see spiritually. Now I was climbing up; I was no longer at the bottom of the valley.

During that ten-week period of confronting all the different kinds of abuse I suffered, I realized that the more I exposed the darkness, the wider the division grew between my husband and me.

Each time he chose to do things as a carnal Christian, he moved further away from God and from me. It was like a mountain splitting from top to bottom. No one can pluck us out of the Lord's hand (*John 10:28-29*), but we can make a decision to walk away from Him. I witnessed it clearly, and sad as it was I could do nothing. I was not Clint's savior. I chose to raise a standard in our home for righteousness; he tore it down repeatedly.

A divided house will fall: *Matthew 12:25* says, "...*Every kingdom divided against itself is brought to desolation: and every city or house divided against itself shall not stand.*" Amos 3:3 says, "*Can two walk together, except they be agreed?*" God won't violate our free will. That's how much He loves us.

God has left the decision up to us to serve Him or deny Christ. If we are lukewarm he will spew us out of his mouth: "*So then because thou art lukewarm, and neither cold nor hot, I will spue thee out of my mouth,*" (Revelation 3:16).

Eternity is a long, long time and I choose to spend it with Jesus, not with the devil. I for sure have had enough of the devil's buffeting on this earth while I am just passing through to my hometown ... Heaven.

Daily I had to practice resisting anger in my own heart, and I had to refuse to take the bait. Throughout this ordeal, I felt abandoned by the church as well as by my husband. I was determined that history would not repeat itself; that I would do something different. **The more I applied the Word of God to my life, the greater my victory in every area of my life.**

Only Jesus can satisfy the heartsick soul. I guess that's why others weren't there for me. He wanted me to come to Him. He helped me get all of this out of my spirit through writing this book. It is harder to get it out of my spirit than into yours. Whose shoes would you rather be in?

# 27. A SUPERNATURAL PUNCH

IN THE NATURAL, IT SEEMED A waste of time to just be cleaning house, reading the Word and praying while the bills piled up and foreclosure kept approaching daily, yet God did not tell me to do anything different. I stretched out on the bed and waited to hear from God. He knew my heart, and it was still and peaceful. Yet as a child needs reassurance, this woman needed reassurance from her Heavenly Father, and I got it. I heard six words from such a powerfully strong yet gentle voice, *"Your best years are not over."*

His words uplifted my spirit, yes, but first there was such a deep, deep hurt, it felt like a twelve-inch needle had been injected into my spirit. I cried out in agony, and then rested. As I lay there I asked God why, when the words were so edifying, was there such hurt and pain. This is what He revealed to me.

He showed me dressed in camouflage as a soldier in His army, and when the words of truth hit my spirit they first had to pierce through a lot of debris. That is why it felt like a twelve-inch needle being injected. The truth, the light, pierced through first, shattering the debris that was causing so much pain. The debris had accumulated over a period of nearly eleven years. In the spirit realm I saw debris that was symbolized by shrapnel—literal debris that had pierced my spirit again and again as grenades were exploding in my face.

They were grenades of anger, fear, and torment; and mental, emotional, and physical abuse. Each time there was more abuse—whether it was emotional, mental or physical—my spirit was pierced with arrows and poison darts.

Yet more verbal abuse; and each demeaning, hurtful word brought more debris my way until I was completely weighed down. I saw what was like a clay-like substance covering me. As it dried the weight of it increased until in my spirit I felt like curling into the fetal position. Yet I couldn't even do that because the clay had hardened on the exterior to the degree I could hardly walk.

I was unrecognizable because of all the pieces of spiritual mortar, arrows, darts, slashes, bruises—many, many bruises—and wounds. The splashes of mud, slander, and lies that hit me had hardened, resulting in a thick—very thick—coat of armor. Yet rather than protecting me, it weighed me down. The real me was unrecognizable. There were so many layers of abuse over the years that had caused much death, because life and death are in the power of the tongue (*Proverbs 18:21*), and so very many awful words had been spoken.

My esteem was smothered, like a candle that had slowly burned out. My identity was gone. I was merely existing; unhappy, deceived, and a soldier that God could not use further until healing was manifested.

When I felt the pain of the words the Lord spoke to me, He also showed me a huge chunk of the clay-like substance break loose from my neck and chest. It was so heavy, like a metal breastplate that cracked and fell free. My body had no strength at that moment, so I just lay there waiting on God, and He gave me this understanding. It was awesome.

He is the Master Surgeon, and even though I had just been through major surgery, I did not have any scars. I saw it all in the spirit realm. God's Word tells us that He reveals things by His Spirit. It is so true. "*But God hath revealed them unto us by his Spirit: for the Spirit searcheth all things, yea, the deep things of God,*" (*1Corinthians 2:10*).

I phoned my prayer partner and shared what had happened. As I talked it out, more understanding came. I knew that if God healed me of everything all at once, it would kill me. He was giving me understanding, and even though it was very painful when the healing took place, it made me want to seek Him for more healing because of the understanding He gave me. I wanted to be completely free.

This was one reason God had me in that house alone, comfortable, quiet, and in His presence. He knew my heart and He was answering my prayers. He dealt with the issues in order of priority, and the first priority was healing. I did not want anything in my life that would hinder me from being used by God to glorify Him. I wanted my life to bring glory to Him, regardless of my marital status. So, He healed me within.

I looked at some photographs of myself that had been taken about four or five years earlier. When I saw the physical changes in myself it was a shock. I knew I was not aglow like I used to be, and I had been asking God, "*Where is my glow? What is wrong?*" I wanted that glow back! Even though I had been in prayer and in the Word steadily—and almost exclusively—for over four months (made possible because I was unemployed!), the glow was not there.

I wanted to know why. The glow of a coal oil lamp cannot shine through when the glass shade is covered with soot, smoke and debris of all sorts. Although the light within is bright and flawless, it cannot be seen clearly because the shade needs to be cleaned—to be healed, if you will. Thus, God was healing me from the damage of abuse over many years.

He showed me that when verbal abuse came and I did not resist it, my spirit got wounded. I did come against the negative words, but they continued so I stopped in an effort to avoid an argument. I knew I could not change my husband so I felt doomed to put up with the abuse. Also, since I did not believe abuse was grounds for divorce, I endured. God knew my heart, my motive, and the deception I was in, but that did not protect my spirit. The wounds still came, and I had been afflicted many, many times. Each time it was as if someone threw mud at a bride in her wedding gown. Once I was out of denial concerning the abuse, God could heal me.

He revealed that He had already healed me mentally. I was so edified. My improved mental state was reflected in how I looked after the house. The less clutter and debris in a home, the less the need for help mentally. The more organized the home, the healthier the mental state of the person organizing, generally speaking. No wonder I got so much joy out of simply cleaning the windows in the house. It was symbolic of the healing process that had already begun. My home was a reflection of me because it reflected 'order'. God is a God of order. "*Let all things be done decently and in order,*" (1 *Corinthians 14:40*).

So, what was my goal once the process of healing was well underway? It was this: to be shiny and squeaky clean by continually washing myself with the water of the Word of God. "*That he might sanctify and cleanse it with the washing of water by the word,*" (*Ephesians 5:26*). I cleansed myself with the blood of Jesus and sought God for any healing I still needed. I wanted God to remove all that was hindering me from serving Him one hundred percent. I had already emerged from the cocoon, and now the transformation was taking place prior to my emergence with a new name: Author.

God is no respecter of persons (*Acts 10:34*), so if He is showing you that you need healing, invite the process to begin so you can be free too. He's got the power, and He is ready and willing to use it in your behalf! Your honesty, though, is required.

# 28. HONESTY

My daddy made real sure of one thing
His children were taught to be honest always
We knew without a doubt
That if we dared lie
We'd be in a heap of trouble
No ifs, buts, or maybes
So I did not lie

In fact, as the years went by
I prided myself on the fact that
Honesty was my policy
Recently, however
God revealed an area of my life
Where I had not been honest
I was astounded and amazed
Then He revealed His viewpoint to me
It was something that only God
Could see

God knew all about the abuse in my life
God knew about the fear, abandonment, rejection
Through the eleven years of abuse
God knew about the constant turmoil
The threats, the attempts made on my life
The betrayal by my husband
So many, many times
Yet God knew I was in much denial

The truth hurt so much
Yet to be in denial is dishonest
That is reality
It was God's love that broke through
Receiving truth is a breakthrough

The truth hurts immensely
Yet knowing the truth
Is what set me free
I can now face reality
God loves me too much
To leave me the way I was
Withdrawn and shriveling up inside
Because of the abuse I received

Isolation was a way to hide
Yet God wants His children healed
Healed and made whole
So He destroyed satan's grip of deception
And kept revealing truths to me

As I sought the Lord
He continued to minister healing to me
God is love and wants me treated accordingly
He is walking me step by step
Out of the eleven-year valley of heartache and suffering
Leading me to a high mountain top
Where with Him I'll stand
And stand tall and unashamedly
Knowing God saw it all and loved me enough

To set me free
And that's
REALITY

To God be the glory

*"For there is nothing covered that shall not be revealed: neither hid, that shall not be known" (Luke 12:2).*

# 29. BELIEVE IT OR NOT

When I think of all the people
Living in this whole wide world
More than I could count
Or even imagine
It is humbling to realize
That God has a plan for me
Personally
Not to mention everyone else (*Jeremiah 29:11*)

It is easy to feel insignificant
Like one grain of sand on the beach
Surrounded by millions of grains
Yet each grain of sand
Is equal in importance
In God's eyes
Together they form a beach
Individually, they may appear insignificant

Yet when a life has been touched by God
That grain of sand no longer lies still
Basking in the sun day by day
The Christ-centered life springs into action
Jumping up and down, dancing
Under the warm rays of the sun
Because resurrection life is on the inside
And it is something one cannot hide

That's why it is so important to know
God's plan for you, personally
He will unfold it bit by bit
By the power of His Spirit
Revelation knowledge will come to you
You'll also have a desire to do
What He calls you to do
God will tell you His plan *(Colossians 1:9)*
Then confirm it by two or more witnesses *(Matthew 18:16)*


Jesus is calling you higher
To a higher realm spiritually
A higher thought life mentally
A deeper walk of faith
A greater commitment of consecration
A more refined speech and more of the Word spoken
As you sing, speak, pray
And teach the Word of God


The Lord has been preparing you for some time
A platform has been prepared too
God has gone before you and prepared the way
In fact, He made a way where there was no way
And now He is calling you ... COME


So step out in faith because believe it or not
You are ready RAINBOW
(Rainbow is my nickname.)
(God says to me, "*You are an extension of my promise ... to others.*")

# 30. ARE YOU GOING TO WALK WITH ME?

I CRAWLED INTO BED AND HEARD the voice of my best friend—Jesus. He asked, *"Are you going to walk with me?"* I said, *"Yes Lord; I THOUGHT I WAS!"* Then I had a flashback of the vision at the beach. Jesus had carried my husband off and I was still standing at the shoreline.

Pain pierced through my soul as I realized I felt like my husband AND Jesus were gone together and I was left standing alone. Yet, I heard myself say, *"I know You are with me,"* as I wiped away the tears.

In my dream, I looked around and could not see Jesus anywhere on the beach. He had called me to walk with Him. I turned around and He was in plain sight standing on the water.

I said, *"The WATER again? Lord, why does it always have to be the WATER?"* Then more tears because I knew He was calling me to walk on the water, to walk with Him, whether on water or land.

I was also aware there was no boat to climb into. The walk started immediately. I didn't feel alone, but I knew I was headed for an eventful journey of faith and prayed I would pass each test. I chose to **"walk with Him"**.

This was also one of the times I had it "backwards" so to speak. I was looking toward the beach where the people were, with Jesus behind me, waiting on the water. He has a special way of ministering to me when something is backwards. This was one of those times, and it was not a coincidence. Jesus really does have a great sense of humor; mine was still being developed. I found that out when I turned around.

Thank God I saw tiny little waves, but I saw NO land behind Jesus, only deep water. My heart filled with love at the thought of being closer to Him. I don't want anything between us. Our communion will be deeper, sweeter, more intimate; it will be all He wants it to be because He has all of my heart, one hundred percent.

My mind wondered what the future held. I also knew the importance of not looking back.

Another thought came. My husband and Jesus were on land; Jesus and I were on the water. **Was this symbolic of walking by faith versus being led by the carnal nature? Now THAT was revelation from God!**

Jesus knows our heart, so he leads each of us accordingly. Walking on water is a higher level spiritually. I knew that the moment my steps left the sandy beach nothing would be as before. I was going to soar to new heights.

As I wrote this, the Lord showed me He and I were going out fishing to bring in others who were in bondage as I was, so we can set them free!

**This book is the fish hook that is baited with love and truth.** Knowing the truth is what sets people free. God loves each of us too much to leave us the way we are. His love, His Word, and the anointing of the Holy Ghost are the ingredients for change in a heart that is yielded accordingly. He does not woo us into a hot skillet over a campfire. Rather, as I learned, He wooed me directly into a fiery furnace!

**The opening of this book is the opening of the fiery furnace beckoning all to enter, yet not without risk. Page by page and chapter by chapter, the fire purges and scales of blindness (spiritual blindness) are removed.** What is a fish without scales? Changed! Readers have an opportunity to experience a refining process that can, with God's help, remove inner struggles and much more, all to the glory of God.

My fiery furnace experiences resulted in the birthing of this book. I wrote whether my spirit, my soul, or my body was in pain. You are reading a first-hand report, hot off the press so to speak, from entry into the fiery furnace to its exit. Each chapter takes you deeper, enabling the Holy Spirit to help you so that you, too, can receive help. This is one furnace that will forever burn because God's refining fire is available to everyone. He can do a fast work with yielded hearts and doesn't even leave a scar. The Master Surgeon works from the inside. **This is an inside job not to be forgotten, yet not to be missed because money cannot purchase such freedom. Praise God!**

**Come ... you are next ...☺**

# 31. ZZZAAAPPPED WITH A PASSWORD

THE FIRE WAS INTENSE, THE PRESSURE was extreme, the furnace was becoming too familiar, yet Divine direction came through. God gets direction through to His children, no matter where they are, because there are no restrictions for Him.

God told me to put the phone in my name solely and to change the password on the account so that only I could make any changes. I obeyed. You see, I was isolated in a rural area with no transportation, and God knew I needed a phone.

Some time earlier Clint had taken my name off the bank accounts without my knowledge, and there was a danger that he would do the same with the phone. But God knows the end from the beginning. Clint reaped what he had sown (*Galatians 6:7*). My Heavenly Father met my need again.

I also believed for money to pay the electric bill. It had been due six days earlier, so I was expecting to get a miracle shortly. I couldn't use the phone or computer, not to mention the central air conditioning (and it sure got hot in Texas), without electricity. I knew that the more the pressure was applied, the closer I was to a miracle. It was that simple! I called in my harvest on seed I had previously planted. He supplies all my needs … in Jesus' Name, (*Philippians 4:19*).

Did I like this time in the furnace? Absolutely NOT! Would it result in bringing glory to God? Absolutely! That was why I was willing to trust God, because He always wins and He is on my side. **When you walk in obedience you are not without troubles, but you are also not without a Good Friend to see you through too—a Friend who sticks closer than a brother.**

*Proverbs 18:24* says, *"A man that hath friends must shew himself friendly: and there is a friend that sticketh closer than a brother."* Jesus is my shelter in every storm. It is wonderful. *"The battle is the Lord's…"* (*1 Samuel 17:47*).

Having peace in my heart is something I was used to having, but it was missing one particular afternoon. I couldn't seem to get a clear direction from God. After getting quiet and praying, He told me what to do. In fact, I realized He had told me not once, but three times. So I made a phone call to the business God told me to call. They informed me that they did not help people with their electric bills anymore and suggested I call the Salvation Army. I did.

After informing them of my situation I learned that after I received a shutoff notice, I was to bring it in with other identification and apply for help. They would try to assist with the bill. They told me to call the electric company.

That made me feel like I was being thrown into the lion's den. I could almost see their open mouths and long white teeth. I tried not to cry and said, "*I really do not want to call them. I do not have a job. I do not have money, and they do not have a lot of compassion. They want money.*" My heart was so heavy.

The lady explained that I needed to know when to expect the shutoff notice, and that I should tell them that the bill would be paid. I thanked her and hung up. I bent over the counter and started to cry. There was so much pressure. Yes, one mountain had lifted—the mountain of the phone—but now there was this one, and there was the land, and the cable, and the Internet, and on and on. Not to mention the house insurance (remember, we lived in "Tornado Alley"). The pressures—financial as well as everything else—were starting to take a toll.

I forced myself to make the call, and also told the Lord I was sorry for complaining because I knew He was helping me. It was humiliating; I felt like I had let the Lord down, hurt my witness, failed—everything was piling in on me.

I called the electric company and spoke to a customer service agent. She listened as I put my cards on the table. I was upfront with her. She told me when to expect the shutoff notice. I thanked her. Then I had to ask another favor.

I told her my husband was trying to force the house into foreclosure. Then I shocked myself when I said, *"I am alive. I live here. I plan to stay. God has never let me down before and He will help me. But under the circumstances, Ma'am, if my husband calls you and tells you to close out this account, is there anything I can do to stop the electricity from being cut off?"*

She said, *"Well there is nothing I can do if he asks us to shut it off."* Then I heard a paper rattle, and sensed a hesitation. She said, *"He is the primary name on the account, but you are on it as his wife."* I said, *"Yes, I am his wife."* She said in a somewhat lower, softer tone, *"Well, you could put a password on the account since you are the wife."*

I thought my knees would buckle. I said, *"I will use one."* I told her what it would be, and she verified it. Then I asked her, *"Does this mean that if he asks to shut off the electricity it won't happen because he won't know the password?"* She said, *"Yes, that is right."* I said, *"Ma'am, you have lifted a lot of pressure off of me. Thank you so much."*

I hung up and saw a scripture, like a ticker tape, running across my forehead saying, *"Behold, I will do a new thing: now it shall spring forth; shall ye not know it? I will even make a way in the wilderness, and rivers in the desert,"* (Isaiah 43:19). Then I saw *Revelation 3:8, "I know thy works: behold, I have set before thee an open door, and no man can shut it: for thou hast a little strength, and hast kept my word, and hast not denied my name."*

I knew that God had opened a door that man could not close. Thank you Jesus! I kept thanking Jesus as I danced into the living room. **God had done it again. He had given me another tripleheader: two months rolled over on the house, followed up with my husband not being able to shut off the phone or the electricity!!!**

God was doing exactly what He told me He would do. He was showing my husband that He, God, was in control, not man. Hallelujah! Glory to

God! Things were certainly not dull in that fiery furnace. Scriptures were coming alive more and more, especially about sowing and reaping. I could tell my husband was going to have an opportunity to get offended big-time. Then I thought about his anger and wondered if I would be in danger. It was not a good thought. I needed to stop that cycle of expectation. I decided not to entertain that thought.

God had protected me that far, and He does not change. Besides that, I was NOT staying in that furnace forever! *"Am I Lord?!!!"*

All these breakthroughs were so good they bear repeating, especially since they bring glory to God. So grasp the truth of God's favor on my life and remember that if suffering is allowed, it won't be in vain. Not when your heart is to serve God, so be encouraged. **If Anyone ... can bring you through ... it is GOD!!**

# 32. FOOTPRINTS IN THE FURNACE

I FELT UNEASY BUT I WAS not sure why. It had been quite a day though, so when the phone rang I wondered what was up now. Sure enough, both people that had provided me a ride to church were not able to do so that night. For a second I questioned if God was having me stay home for any particular reason, especially since I was feeling edgy and did not get like that very often, or without a reason. I thought about it briefly. Since I knew my husband wanted our Miniature Schnauzer, Dan, I also knew there was a possibility he would try to break in and get him when I was at church.

However, as much as I loved the dog, I decided I could not live in that kind of fear where I couldn't even leave the house in case my husband came to steal him. So I decided to go to church and not worry about Clint and what he might do. I was just not going to stay home. I asked God to help me get a ride.

After making one phone call I had a ride arranged and was praising God for meeting my need. This couple had such a great attitude too, even though I lived several miles out of their way. Attitude means so much. If someone provides a ride for me and their attitude is not good I would rather stay home. A good deed done with no heart involvement is not very good fruit. Praise God I was on the receiving end of love from a sincere, warm Christian couple.

Just before I left the house, since there was such uneasiness in my spirit, I decided to take whatever precautions I could to prevent my husband from being able to just enter the house at random. I knew he had a key for one lock on the front door, so I decided to make sure the dead bolt was on so he could not get in. We were separated, and it was a violation to come in when I was not there.

Then I made sure the patio door was locked and even went so far as to put a long stick in the bottom track so he could not get the door open. I left by the back door and used the key with the dead bolt because he did not have a key for it. That was the best I could do. So I left for church knowing the dog might not be barking for me when I returned. I tried not to think about it. I just wanted to go to church and was not going to stay home in case my husband came. I decided to put God first.

Obedience always pays good dividends. Church was wonderful. I would not have wanted to miss it. Learning how to enter into the secret place with my heavenly Father was something I wanted to learn for sure. When I returned home I headed for the backyard. As I opened the gate I got a sick feeling in my stomach and looked at the patio door. The dog was not barking.

The vertical blinds were not waving at me from Dan's pushing them open with his little nose. I looked at the window panes in the back door and was relieved to see they were intact. I listened for the dog, still feeling heartsick as I put my key in the dead bolt. As I entered the house I knew before I called out to Dan that he was gone.

I walked through the kitchen; the patio door appeared okay, and the stick was still in place. I approached the front door and immediately saw that the dead bolt had been turned and was unlocked. Fear attacked me at that instant because I realized someone took the dog, and it did not necessarily mean it was my husband. What if it was someone else and that person was in the house with me at that very moment? It was unnerving.

I recognized the enemy and said, "*... satan, I bind you; I rebuke fear in Jesus' Name. Go.*" I proceeded to check the door. The front door handle lock had been reset so that it was locked when the intruder left.

The bedroom doors were shut as I had left them. I entered each room and everything appeared to be in place. But the dog was gone, and so was his water dish. Then I saw spots of water on the carpet spilled from the dish when it was taken. There was a bit of water on the kitchen floor too. I remembered the neighbors to the south being outside when I left. I wondered if they had seen the intruder approach and leave. They knew we were separated. I decided not to go over. I needed to think. It was beginning to be a very long day.

I phoned a friend, and as we were talking I noticed a note on the kitchen table as well as a single key. The note said, **"Linda, I have Dan. Clint."** The key was placed on top of the note. Kind of said it all.

I thought to myself, he broke in and entered the house, yet I couldn't even call the law because it was his house too, even though we were separated. What sense was it for him to leave the key unless it was so I would not call the police? He broke in and did not use the key. However, I discovered the patio door could simply be lifted several inches straight up and slid open! If you have patio doors, you might want to check them out, just in case.

More thoughts came to me. People reap what they sow (*Galatians 6:7*). When someone puts me under a lot of pressure, the same will come back on that person. Not necessarily in the same way, but pressure will be applied. It is a Bible principle. I started to feel some anger and right away I said out loud, *"No devil, I am not giving in to that anger. You are not stealing my peace. I am not even going to cry over this. At least I am not co-dependent on the dog. God is my protector, not the dog, so I will be fine."*

More thoughts started to bombard my mind. The enemy tried to return with fear by saying, *"You are here alone now … everyone knows your husband is gone … you do not have a car … you are a target now … you do not have any protection."* I did not take long to put a stop to those words. They were not going to take root in my mind. I took authority spiritually and put a stop to the lies of the devil.

I had peace in my heart as I made sure everything else was in order. Then I remembered feeling edgy and nervous when I left the house to go to church. I sensed something was wrong yet had peace about leaving, so I did. I believe I was picking up the nervousness Clint was feeling as he waited for me to leave the house.

He was obviously watching the house when I left and then made his move. It is a bit unnerving to think someone is watching your moves in your own home. It surprised me that fear kept trying to get a foot in the door, but I did not let that happen. Then I thought about Dan and tried not to cry. I told myself that I would see him again.

As I was choking back tears the Lord spoke something so precious to me. He said, **"You made a quality decision when you chose to go to church. You put Me first. That is good fruit."** Then the tears DID come! The Lord knows exactly what to say and when to say it, and in such a loving tone too. I smiled, brushed away the tears, and thanked Him for making me strong and for preparing me.

Then I released forgiveness to my husband. I was surprised I did not feel more anger towards him, but it just was not there. I recognized the spiritual battle, so getting angry at him would not solve anything. I forgave him and asked God to deal with him. I knew Clint would reap what he had sown; how he dealt with me was how God would deal with him because God is just. This is the principle of sowing and reaping: *"Be not deceived; God is not mocked: for whatsoever a man soweth, that shall he also reap. For he that soweth to his flesh shall of the flesh reap corruption; but he that soweth to the Spirit shall of the Spirit reap life everlasting, (Galatians 6:7-8).*

I had never in the past refused to let my husband take the dog with him when he asked, not even one time. To cause such pain was cruel. He acted out of his own fear of not getting the dog. I tried to keep my eyes on the Lord. *"… My grace is sufficient…" (2 Corinthians 12:9).*

Then more thoughts came: *"Clint fears going to jail and being in a confined area … what if the police charge him with break and enter? That sure would be a lot of pressure for him. Yet look at the pressure he has put me under. I sure am glad I have peace. But what if they can charge him with break and enter? This is very serious. I do not know what would happen. What about his CDL (Commercial Driver's License)? Maybe he would have to retire early, but can the law do anything without a legal separation? Oh, my stomach. I can just imagine his fear if the law stops him and he is in the truck. Maybe the law will bring the dog back to me if he gets arrested."*

I didn't even want to think about it all. It was all I could do to type my notes for this book, but it was done, so I entered into communion with my Heavenly Father. He always knows exactly what to say and do.

I remembered that when I was fretting about the phone bill and the electric bill that day there was a moment of frustration when I said, ***"Lord, I am sweating, I have tears, but You are not sweating and You have no tears. Yet we are in this furnace together. How come?"*** Then we started to laugh. Later that evening I thought about that moment and realized Jesus had no stress and no fear. He had total confidence in the Father and so He had no reason to sweat or shed tears.

As for me, I had not yet come to fully trust God to supply all my needs as He promised. I needed to enter into the complete peace Jesus paid the price for me to have. No matter how hot it got in the furnace, I was not ever alone. I didn't like the furnace one bit, but I knew Jesus was carrying me while I was in it. He certainly carried my burdens. They were not for me to carry. The footprints in the furnace, for sure, were His. Praise the Lord. Now that is a good idea for a new song, *Footprints In The Furnace.*

## 33. WHEN IS THE LAST TIME?

When is the last time
You cried yourself to sleep
I wonder if there is anyone
In the whole world
That has never experienced this

Last night was heart wrenching
Absolutely grievous indeed
I slept periodically
Yet my heart did bleed
A lot

I awoke knowing
Nothing would be the same
It was like a death
Yet my dog
Was alive

It doesn't matter how spiritual
Anyone is
They are not shielded from pain
Suffering a loss like this
Is a deep wound to the spirit

I do not want pity from others
I just want to rise above the pain
It is awful, just awful

How does anyone call himself a Christian
Yet bring such suffering to another

Most people hurt
When they hurt someone else
This man feels good
When he hurts me
Repeatedly

More patience gained
Hopefully
Suffering is no fun
Can he really have his cake
And eat it too

I choose to place my trust
In God and He will help me
Whether I am abandoned and betrayed
By people
God is with me

Some day justice will be served
For now I will look up
Press on, not quit
Just spend time in the secret place
The unseen realm is more real to me than what I see

*"It Won't Rain Always"
So the song title says
Memories help, so does prayer

Especially when friends seem to have disappeared
Yet they are busy ... somewhere

Thank God it has been such a long time
Since I cried myself to sleep
Repeatedly
At least I can find something
To be thankful for

I just pray it will be a long, long, long time
Before I ever cry myself to sleep again
This was enough to last me for a lifetime
Besides, I choose life, not heartache
So I know God is for me; He's the Author of life

**\*Song Title: "It Won't Rain Always"**
**Written By: Bill And Gloria Gaither and Aaron Wilburn**

The rain in my heart stopped, then it was Clint's turn. He called me in tears a few weeks after taking the dog to tell me I needed to take care of him. He said the cat where he was living scratched the dog's eye and surgery had been required.

I said, **"Nope."** His tears turned to anger as he shouted, **"WHY?"** I said, **"Because he's YOUR DOG!"** Then I hung up. I think it was the fastest decision I ever made. Plus it was not followed by tears; only peace. I saw God's sowing and reaping principle at work. Stunning! **If you dish it out, be prepared for payback somehow. To mess with God's servants is unwise.**

# 34. A NEW VIEWPOINT

Some people can relate
To a fiery furnace experience
Spiritually, but not all
Some give words of well-meaning advice
Resulting in pressure being intensified
Rather than providing some relief

When I am told I need to generate some income
Then someone else tells me to do something
To run
Yet is no more specific than that
I do not get edified

When I took those comments to the Lord
He led me to read something
That made sense and helped me a lot
At least it showed me the importance
Of obeying God, daring to be different

First I recognized peace in my heart
So I knew all was well
If I am to be doing something else
And I am not
There is no peace

The Lord led me to read this
*"You are learning not to tell every experience.*
*Never speak without My guidance.*
*Be content to share with Me alone*
*Until you have My clear direction."*

God has a reason for directing me this way
Many people do not have ears to hear
The world's doubt and skepticism
Has an undermining influence
On my faith

My testimony can be used
To help many people
But only in God's timing
So I need to be content to wait
Until God sends me forth

Consequently, I decided to make a change
I'll speak but to very few
About what I am going through
Everyone can read it when this is published
Till then, I'll do more pondering

Maybe the reason there are so few people
In this furnace with me
Is because they can't take the heat
Yet for gold to become purified
Much heat must be applied

Whew. Help me Jesus
I asked to become more refined
But don't be surprised
If I don't ask that again for a while
Whew ....... ☺

# 35. MAKING MEMORIES

A LADY FROM CHURCH OFFERED TO drive me to do errands. That helped a lot, as I needed legal advice and had a doctor's appointment. I was given a four-month supply of pills to stop the hot flashes. That was a blessing.

This lady shared with me the fact that she went through a divorce years earlier. She thought God would not be able to use her to do any counseling and was upset about it. God used someone to tell her that He would use her to help a lot of people who were going through divorce. I was one of those people, and it blessed both of us. Praise the Lord.

Next we shopped for groceries. There were four specific items that I needed. I was able to purchase the brand name version of each one, in the size I wanted, and all four were on sale. It was definitely not a coincidence. I do not shop alone; the Holy Spirit leads me and it is a trip to enjoy, full of surprises.

We went out for lunch and had delicious Chinese food. I found myself asking, *"Lord, can all these people afford to eat out?"* I'll let you figure out what the answer was to that question. As for me, I had seven dollars to my name and saw lunch out as a real treat and was thankful.

After lunch we went to my friend's home for a visit and she handed me two sacks of supplies. It was inspiring. She was giving me all kinds of paper goods. Since I was on welfare using a Lone Star card, I could purchase edible groceries but no paper goods. I was given three boxes of tissue, four rolls of toilet paper, half a dozen bars of soap and two extra large rolls of paper towels. But that was not all.

I was looking at a small sales catalog and saw deodorant advertised for ninety-nine cents. That was pretty cheap for two ounces, so I asked my friend if she ever tried it. She looked at me, her mouth dropped open, she headed for the kitchen pantry and I heard her ask, *"What kind of deodorant do you use?"* I told her. She gave me the thumbs up. I think my mouth was open at that point. I thought to myself, *"Hello, Hello!"* I just knew God was up to something good, and my friend and her husband had Him on the line that is never busy!

She walked back in the living room carrying a new roll-on deodorant in my brand and gave it to me. She told me her husband picked it up that morning when they were putting some things together for me, and then they thought maybe deodorant was too personal. **NOT!!! We had a good laugh over that and know the Lord was smiling too. It becomes too personal when you don't have any!!!**

We were in the car and my friend said, *"Now, this may not be too good for our waistlines but I'd like to have some ice cream."* My mouth definitely dropped open then. I had been craving ice cream for weeks but couldn't afford it. Again, I knew it was not a coincidence; God knew the desires of my heart, and hers too. So we enjoyed every calorie!

I sure hope and pray that you are able to recognize that the Holy Spirit was leading us step by step that day, and it was a very special day of happy memories. *"A merry heart doeth good like a medicine: but a broken spirit drieth the bones,"* (Proverbs 17:22). God knew I needed to have some "fun," and my friend needed a nice day too. Her only brother had passed away very suddenly just a few weeks earlier and she was grieving. When she left she was smiling though, and so was I.

God touches hearts effectively. *Isaiah 55:8, 9* says, *"For my thoughts are not your thoughts, neither are your ways my ways, saith the* LORD. *For as the heavens are higher than the earth, so are my ways higher than your ways, and my thoughts than your thoughts."*

God knows exactly what women need. God knows what men need. God is still God whether you are in the valley or on a mountaintop. His ways are higher. His thoughts are wiser. I am so glad!

I might add that my friend was concerned about how it might affect me when I saw her dog, since mine had been taken only two days earlier. I was deeply touched by her thoughtfulness and compassion. I was absolutely fine. It did not bother me at all. In fact, I had to thank God because I realized I had been completely healed with regard to the loss of the dog. All pain was gone, and I knew the tears I had shed all night long when it happened, as well as forgiving Clint for taking the dog, are what made my healing a fast process. God did not want me, or anyone, walking around with a bunch of hurts sticking out here and there like poison darts. Healing is our right, now.

By the time the evening rolled around I had received so much love and such a refreshing, I started to mow my lawn. God had supernaturally strengthened me with the spirit of might and power. His unconditional love never fails. It sure had been a great day! Memories are made of this kind of love. Memories of God's love flowing freely touching hearts and meeting needs. Praise God for this Divine appointment.

In contrast, there were other times when being on the receiving end was not nearly as much of a blessing. Once only I went to my church and received a check to help me when I moved. When it was handed to me I was told very sternly, and with no smile, *"This is GOD's money. You take CARE of God's money."*

I discerned that this person did not think I should be receiving the check and was giving begrudgingly. It surprised me because in my heart I was saying to God, *"EVERYTHING I have is Yours Lord. I am just a steward of it. Everything I receive is from You, Lord, not just this. I do not receive any condemnation though. Thank you Lord."*

This scripture came to mind: *"Every good gift and every perfect gift is from above, and cometh down from the Father of lights, with whom is no variableness, neither shadow of turning,"* (James 1:17). I was as thankful for that check as I was for any check, or even for an ice cream sundae. I knew God was my Source. It made the receiving much easier, though, if it was given in love—given without pride, judgment, or begrudgingly; not to mention a religious spirit.

Thank God He sees our hearts, and I was so glad. It was the first and last time I ever received money through that church. I trusted God to provide for me and never had to ask anyone ever again. My faith went to another level. I prayed that the person who handed me that check would mature too so other people would be protected from such an attitude. When I was bought the ice cream sundae, if I had been told, **"This is GOD's ice cream,"** I think I would have had a hard time swallowing it! Thank God for the humble attitude of His servants that blessed me with groceries, hospitality, fellowship, transportation, time and compassion; and in doing so did it ALL with much unconditional love. Their fruit was flawless!

There was no shame when I received from them. They were Christ's hand extended to me in love. I was uplifted and greatly encouraged. Oh, that more Christians would have such a wonderful attitude. No one wants to suffer from poverty and shame. Not anyone. I was a victim with needs and a woman who did not ask to be in that position.

My husband broke covenant with me and his choices affected me adversely. Yet I was just childlike enough to believe that God did not place me at the bottom of the totem pole, so to speak. The Bible says *"... God is no respecter of persons," (Acts 10:34).* He loves me as much as He loves any well-known preacher or a homeless person living in an alley or under a bridge.

When I was forgiven of much—and I was—my love for God became much and it has continued to increase as I continue to become more like Him. Praise God. This is my prayer for you too: *"... Her sins, which are many, are forgiven; for she loveth much; but to whom little is forgiven, the same loveth little," (Luke 7:47).*

**Honesty is key with me ... so I stayed true to God's restoration process for me. The more of God's Word I read and studied, the more restored I became. It happened as I was still IN the fiery furnace, so to speak.** It was months before the Lord led me to move out. It was during those months of pressure that this book was written. God's delay was not a denial, nor was it without a purpose ... because He is God.

# 36. IN HIM I PLACE MY TRUST

At a time when one thing I need
Is a friend
It seems my new friend will move
Our blessed time together will end
Maybe this is God's way
Of showing me
It is the Lord only that I can lean on
That's the way it has to be

It hurts
She and I phone each other and chat
We help each other too
That's where it's at
She picks me up, as I don't have a car
I baby sit occasionally, call her too
We fellowship and are at ease
It's just something God did do

I have three other friends
I know much better
Yet I don't see them but a few times a year
May as well just write a letter
It is not good for me to have a pity party
Especially when I know God has a plan
He won't abandon me
I'll just hold tightly to His hand

He will lead me step by step
He will comfort and encourage me
He will wipe away my tears
He will help me see spiritually
I am to lean on the Lord
I simply must
He's there 24/7
In Him, I place my trust

# 37. WHY THIS DEATHLY SILENCE?

What happened
To people who take note
When they hear someone has a need
They hear a friend has no car, no job, no money
Yet that friend speaks words of life, faith
Even encouragement to others
But when it comes to reaching out to her
It just doesn't happen much at all

Could it be they forgot you have needs
Could it be they refused to get involved
Could it be they are in such bondage
They can't spare gas for your lawnmower
Or a jug of milk, loaf of bread, some meat
Yet if someone dies
Along come the casserole dishes
To the front door......hmmm

How about offering a trip to the grocery store
Or even just a ride
After spending weeks on end
Inside.....
Is it too much of a bother
To include just one more person occasionally
Not to mention a dinner invitation some Sunday
Is it too easy to look the other way

What happened to people
Who are willing to go the extra mile
And with a good attitude as well
Seems they are few and far between
I searched my heart about all this treatment
Or lack thereof....
Wondered if I was reaping what I sowed
Thankfully, God ministered to me

He reminded me of times I provided transportation
Times I invited people home for dinner
And for fellowship too
Bags of groceries I gave away
Many boxes of clothing too
Household items, cash, and furniture also
It wasn't a lot
But I did what I could do

Not to mention gifts for children and adults
An open door and a welcome mat to them too
A glass of water to a thirsty trash seeker
Money for others when God told me to
There wasn't anything I wouldn't do
I did it as unto the Lord and He knew
Friendship was extended sincerely
So why this deathly silence in my home now

One person phones me every single day
She's at the opposite end of town but keeps in touch
'Cause she knows the fire is hot

It is a trial I'm going through
She knows God is helping me
Says she does not want a trial like this
However, she's learning a lot, and is a great
Sounding board for me

She knows when my faith is strong
She knows if I'm up or down
She knows the importance of speaking words of life
Speaking things that be not as though they were (*Romans 4:17*)
Not trying to figure it all out
Not griping, complaining, and murmuring
Decisions are made each day
Resulting in fruit in my life, good or bad

Good fruit is when I write
Though my flesh does not want to
Being this transparent is intimidating
Makes me want to get the book published
Then retreat, hibernate
Leave the gold fish bowl empty
Because I don't want everyone talking about me
Yet they are anyway so God said, ***"Keep writing."***

Consequently I'm not peeking one day
Past the last page of this book
I just know I'm to obey God
So I'll get the job done
As for my being alone so much
I find several people phone periodically

Because they want an update
They don't really reach out to help me

I lowered my expectations
Am not expecting anything from anyone
My Source is the Lord, my eyes are on Him
My communion with Him is more intimate
He never abandons me
I pray for God to help people reach out more
The mission field is where you see a need
I pray I don't get too self-centered to help others

I've planted lots of seed in fertile soil
I'm confessing the Word and believing it too
God will not let me down, it's Harvest Time
I, by faith, am debt free
God honors obedience, faithfulness, tithing and giving
God honors His Word
So the end result: what happened to all those people
Does not matter ........ Jesus is here

*Praise the Lord for Luke 6:38; Malachi 3:10,11;*
*Deuteronomy 1:11; Jeremiah 29:11-14.*

# 38. AS UNTO HIM

I mowed and I mowed and I mowed the grass
Prayed in the spirit too
Told myself it was good to do this
Because my home is God's home
He lives here too
I cleaned the house and mowed the yard as unto Him

My legs were tired
My feet were sore
My hands threatened to blister as well
It was hot and humid
But I prayed and God answered

He gave me the spirit of strength and might
He supernaturally strengthened me
For seven hours I walked and mowed
I was in my fifties and didn't exercise much
Yet when a job needs to get done
And there's no one else to help
I can do all things through Christ
Who strengthens me (Philippians 4:13)

He did it today
The house is clean
The yard looks good too
Yet it's just the Lord and me here
On a Saturday night

Peace and tranquility
Works for me

I am tired, but happy
I hear a dog barking in the distance
A train whistle as well
The neighbor's children must be in bed
There's not a voice to be heard
Except for the voice within me
He just whispered so softly
**"I'm here."**

When you know Jesus
When you have a personal relationship with Him
You've got the Best Friend ever
None can compare even slightly
He appreciates everything I do
I found out little things mean a lot
To Him too

Praise the Lord

# 39. TRANSPARENT HEART

I heard myself say something today
That I never thought I would ever say
So with a transparent heart I'll tell you

Through tears I said, "Lord,
*Take me to Heaven now, I just want to die.*
*I don't want to be here anymore."*
He was silent. I continued:
*"I don't want to go even one step without You.*
*I don't even think I can continue WITH You.*
*I can't take any more.*
*Just take me home."*

More tears as I buried my head in my pillow
Immediately I heard five words
**"I'm going to do something."**
Then he repeated it
**"I'm going to do something."**

Let me tell you how those five words affected me
They had the same calming effect one receives
The moment hail ceases completely
And I knew in my knower
He would do something
It would not be simply "lip service"

I don't know what He'll do, but I don't have to know
If anyone knows what He's doing, He does
And He never fails
So even though the fire is hot
I'm so glad to be with Jesus
My trust is in Him
That's why my heart can be transparent
I can be real
Because He is real in my life

If I remain transparent
Then you can see Jesus
In me
"*... Christ in me the hope of glory,*" (*Colossians 1:27*)
That's what it is all about anyway, isn't it

# 40. SOCIAL RESTORATION

I WAS A BIT APPREHENSIVE ABOUT attending my church's annual picnic even though I am a people person. I was looking forward to getting out of the house and was thankful to be going with another family, yet I was apprehensive for a good reason.

I knew I didn't really fit in with the singles because I was still married, yet since I was alone I was not sure how the couples would react to me as I reached out. I prayed and asked God to put me in contact with the people He wanted me in contact with and to guide the conversation, because I did not want to be a burden to anyone.

I spread my blanket on the green grass, parked my chair and sat down. It was sunny and windy but really nice, not too hot. A couple sat near me. The wife, who I had met briefly at church before, asked me a question. We started to visit, her husband as well, and we visited throughout dinner. They were friendly and I was thankful. I had not met her husband before.

Then another woman passed by and greeted us. We started visiting and she commented on the t-shirt I was wearing. It had a Christian message, and she said she really liked it, so I gave her the business card of a friend of mine who sold the shirts. She thanked me and moved on, and soon after the other couple left.

I sat there looking around. Suddenly I felt like I did not know anyone. I had only been going to this church for about two or three months. (My husband had changed churches again. He only went to this one once and then quit. That is when I made a decision not to church hop anymore, so I went alone.)

As I sat there, I felt the wonderful presence of the Lord. At the same time, I recognized that my mind was being attacked by lies of the enemy telling me I was alone. I was not alone. Besides, I knew how to be friendly and decided it was time for me to reach out. If you want friends you have to be friendly.

I headed toward a young lady my daughter's age. I had met her elsewhere and knew she had just started attending this church too. We visited a bit, then I got my chair and joined her and another friend of hers, and I met her children too. We ladies visited and I enjoyed watching the children use the park playground facilities. I had an opportunity to touch base with my pastors, and that was a blessing because they were always so busy and had so many people to see.

Next a friend came and told me about a particular couple that she wanted me to talk to. I went over and did so. The couple was involved in ministry, helping others in the area of financial counseling. I asked some questions and they helped me, even though our time together was brief.

Before long it was time to go home, and I was tired but glad I had attended the picnic. Nothing exciting had really happened, but in a way I was excited. I was getting back into circulation. Isolation is not good. I was reaching out too, not willing to sit and wait for people to come to me. I wasn't content to stay home because of some preconceived idea that church picnics are boring. I was glad I had not stayed home and I made a mental note to go next year too.

As for the conversation, I did share with a few people what had happened concerning my marriage and I knew it was a new release for me, a healing taking place as light walked into the darkness. No one condemned me, and some even showed me compassion. That touched my heart and allowed more of the hurt to come out. Praise the Lord.

On the other hand, I did not want to be badmouthing my husband. The things that had happened were past, and I just wanted to get on with my life and not be bitter. I told these people that the hardest thing was keeping my heart right with God, but that was my first priority because bitterness would hurt me more than it would Clint.

The enemy told me people were talking about me and saying my husband just walked out on me. I tried not to let it bother me, but I knew that as time passed more people had become aware. These thoughts were part of the mental battle that went on in my mind from time to time, because the mind is the battleground—the spiritual battleground. I tried not to entertain such negative thoughts that were like darts attacking my mind.

My focus was on the Lord. I believed He was helping me break through from a nonexistent social life with my husband to a new beginning with Jesus as my spiritual husband, and I found out He likes social events. In fact, Jesus became my escort; He was with me all the time, and I knew He would never abandon me. I don't know if others felt His presence as strongly as I did that day, but it was wonderful.

As I looked over the crowd I noticed how some people parked and stayed put. They visited with the few people near them as if there were only about eight or ten people at the park. They did not attempt to mix or get to know other people, to circulate. I wondered what Jesus would do.

Would He sit and isolate Himself with just a few, or would He be looking for the hurting soul, looking for someone to minister to, looking for someone who needs to know he or she is loved? I wondered what He would do. Jesus is our example, and He is not selfish at all, nor is He self-centered. It takes an effort to share our lives with others, and we need to risk hurt, rejection and misunderstandings by being vulnerable.

Jesus was vulnerable. He was transparent. Are you? Whose steps did you follow when you were last with a crowd? Was it Jesus'? Were there but one set of footprints because He was carrying you? Did you follow Him or allow Him to carry you? I dare say that is what happened to me because the Lord made it so easy for me at that picnic. Glory to God.

God gave me some homework to do after the picnic that day. He had me look up some verses and type them out because He wants everyone to praise Him, to sing. **Singing is the protocol for entering the presence of the Holy**

**Spirit.** *Psalm 100:1-5 says, "Make a joyful noise unto the* LORD, *all ye lands. Serve the* LORD *with gladness: come before his presence with singing. Know ye that the* LORD *he is God: it is he that hath made us, and not we ourselves; we are his people, and the sheep of his pasture. Enter into his gates with thanksgiving, and into his courts with praise: be thankful unto him, and bless his name. For the* LORD *is good; his mercy is everlasting; and his truth endureth to all generations."*

He may also nudge us to praise Him by having someone say something to us, or He may prompt us through an email or a letter we receive. No matter what method He uses, when we feel that nudge or prompting to praise Him or sing to Him, we should obey.

I had not been praising the Lord because I had lost my song. It was no wonder the Lord had me look up *Psalm 100* and all the verses that follow. He was telling me I needed to sing, too. Knowing what we are to do, and doing it, is what pleases God. That's obedience. I made a commitment to sing unto Him, and I pray these verses help you as much as they helped me. **No matter what your singing sounds like, it is beautiful to Him.**

(PSALM 105:2) *"Sing unto him, sing psalms unto him: talk ye of all his wondrous works."*

(PSALM 81:1) *"Sing aloud, unto God our strength; make a joyful noise unto the God of Jacob."*

(PSALM 100:2) *"Serve the Lord with gladness: come before his presence with singing."*

(ISAIAH 51:11) *"Therefore the redeemed of the Lord shall return, and come with singing unto Zion; and everlasting joy shall be upon their head: they shall obtain gladness and joy; and sorrow and mourning shall flee away."*

(EPHESIANS 5:19) (Amplified) *"Speak out to one another in psalms and hymns and spiritual songs, offering praise with voices [and instruments], and making melody with all your heart to the Lord."*

(COLOSSIANS 3:16) (Amplified) *"Let the word [spoken by] Christ (the Messiah) have its home [in your hearts and minds] and dwell in you in [all its]* richness, as you teach and admonish and train one another in all insight and intelligence and wisdom [in spiritual things, and as you sing] psalms and hymns and spiritual songs, making melody to God with [His] grace in your hearts."

(1 CHRONICLES 16:9) "Sing unto him. Sing songs unto him, talk ye of all his wondrous works."

(PSALM 13:6) "I will sing to the Lord because he has dealt bountifully with me."

(PSALM 30:4) "Sing unto the Lord, O ye saints of his, and give thanks at the remembrance of his holiness."

(PSALM 96:1) "O sing unto the Lord a new song: sing unto the Lord all the earth."

(PROVERBS 29:6) "In the transgression of an evil man there is a snare: but the righteous doth sing and rejoice."

(ISAIAH 12:5) "Sing unto the Lord; for he hath done excellent things; this is known in all the earth."

(ZEPHANIAH 3:17) (Amplified) "The Lord your God is in the midst of you, a mighty One, a Savior [Who saves]! He will rejoice over you with joy; He will rest [in silent satisfaction] and in His love He will be silent and make no mention [of past sins, or even recall them]; He will exult over you with singing."

**I especially like the last verse knowing GOD SINGS over us! WOW!!**

# 41. RESULTS OF ABANDONMENT

ONE NIGHT THE HOLY SPIRIT INSTRUCTED me to write about a certain experience. I did not want to as I was very tired from all the stress and the heat and did not want to have to relive yet another painful experience. To write about it, I had to relive it. Maybe that was selfish of me, but I also wasn't so sure that my future readers would care about all my painful experiences.

Then a friend told me that others could relate to the pain I experienced. She suggested I write about it so that God could use my experiences to draw the hurt out of other wounded spirits. How could I say no? I couldn't, but it was still very difficult.

This had been a difficult day. I had not gotten to sleep until after 3:30 that morning. I hadn't had a burden to pray about anything or anyone specifically, yet I just could not go to sleep. As the morning wore on, I did pretty well until about 11 a.m. when the fatigue became almost overwhelming and I wanted to go back to bed. So why not, it looked so inviting, and there wasn't much else for me to do.

The things that could be packed were already packed and I didn't have much food left so I didn't even have to think about breakfast. There was no bread, margarine or butter; no crackers or cheese. There was only about a cup of milk, so I made myself a cup of hot chocolate, and that was breakfast. I was too tired to be hungry anyway. I don't mean to complain, just trying to paint an accurate and honest picture of what my life was like that day.

I was glad that there were two people coming that afternoon with a car to help me move and I was thinking about what to do next. The storage unit I had rented was full, yet I had more things to move so I called and got the price of another, smaller unit. The problem was, I only had thirty-five cents to my name.

I didn't want to use a credit card, but since help was coming that afternoon and I had to have a place to put my stuff, I called to verify that the storage company would accept credit cards. Back then, they usually wouldn't accept credit for storage units, but they made an exception for me. Once again, God gave me favor with man. I paid the $35 fee, plus the $25 deposit. Now storage was costing me a total of $95 each month.

God knew my heart, and putting my things in storage was definitely not my heart's desire, but I reminded myself that it was just a temporary situation.

Everything went well with the move and I felt relieved that I had gotten more of it out of the way. The bedroom furniture and basic necessities were still left and would not take long to move. I had called both the electric and the phone companies and confirmed that both utilities would remain connected until after I moved out. That was certainly a blessing of the Lord because it would appear someone was inside and hopefully be a deterrant against thieves. I had no idea I would be in the house so long after the separation, but I knew God had a purpose.

One purpose was that this chapter, and many of the previous chapters, would not have been written if I had been moved out of the house earlier. Also, God was showing Clint that He, God, was in control! Clint wasn't, nor was I for that matter! God always has a purpose for what He asks us to do. Not that this chapter is a special nugget, but you know what? If it results in helping one person it was worth whatever I went through to bring that help.

I made myself go outside and sit on the back deck. The patio doors were locked and secured more tightly than usual in case of an attempted break-in, so I used the back door. This extra security resulted in my feeling a bit like a prisoner in my own home. It meant I had to make sure I did not lock myself outside. So, being careful not to lock myself out, I grabbed the only lawn chair, my Bible, and headed for the deck. There was one drastic change, though, since the last time I sat out there—the grass had grown about five inches and it was a mess!

I had sold the lawn mower to get much needed cash so I could get a storage building and food, thinking I would move in a few weeks. That was about a month earlier and there had been a lot of rain that month. Even though the grass was much too long, it was nice to see it green. With the hot summer sun in Texas, green grass was a rare sight. At least the green grass looked like there was some life around. I knew there might be a snake in that grass so I put my glasses to good use as I stepped gingerly with sandal-clad feet toward the deck, praying earnestly as I went.

But it was after eight p.m. and the sunset was pretty, so I was able to enjoy that. I started to read, but soon my concentration was disturbed by voices—children's voices coming from a neighbor's yard. I thought about my own grandchildren who were 1600 miles away, and it hurt not seeing them, not hugging them, not having the opportunity to nurture them spiritually.

I tossed those thoughts aside and started to read again. Then I heard a dog barking. I caught myself daydreaming, looking blankly into the long grass, the barking echoing in my mind as I thought about my dog, stolen when I was at church. Ouch, ouch, more ouch. I thought to myself, at least my dog sounded more cheerful.

I made a mental decision not to go there, not to have a pity party over the dog, not to look back at all. Rather, I would refocus. Onward and upward. It was a spiritual battle and I was not going to weaken after coming so far. I breathed in the air. It was not hot; it was very comfortable and I appreciated that, then I heard more voices.

A woman kept calling her dog. I heard a voice say, *"He's not coming."* I sensed the fear in her voice as I heard a car approaching down the road. Next my ears became fine tuned to the shrill whistling again and again in a desperate attempt to lure the dog to safety. It must have worked, because silence resumed.

I tried to read some more, but my mind flashed back to the time the two little girls I wrote about earlier were playing in the backyard. I remembered the joy I had felt hearing their laughter and watching them become friends as they played ball on the freshly mowed lawn. To see my yard now, overgrown and neglected, was like a bad dream. It reeked of abandonment. That was all I could think.

You see, the exterior of a home is a reflection of the interior. It was obvious that nothing had been done to manicure the yard, front or back, and there was not one flower, shrub, or tree. I had hired someone to build a large front verandah, but without a sprinkler system I could not fight the Texas sun to keep the grass green when it was 100 degrees Fahrenheit for weeks on end.

There were no sidewalks, no dog in the yard—there was no life at all. My heart started to tighten as I felt the loneliness try to cover me like a blanket. *"No way,"* I thought, *"I refuse to be lonely."*

*"Jesus,"* I prayed, *"Thank you for grace. Thank you that I am moving onward and upward spiritually. Thank you that you know my heart. The last time I mowed this acreage I did it as unto You and You know it. I am not lazy or tardy. I do not accept the lies of the devil, nor do I accept his condemnation."*

So many scriptures flooded my mind: *"There is therefore now no condemnation to them which are in Christ Jesus, who walk not after the flesh, but after the Spirit,"* (Romans 8:1).

I am walking out of the bondage of mental, emotional, and physical abuse and darkness no longer has a part in my life. I am consumed with the truth! *"And ye shall know the truth, and the truth shall make you free,"* (John 8:32).

I am no longer a victim! *"...in all these things we are more than conquerors through him that loved us,"* (Romans 8:37); *"Greater is He that is in me than he that is in the world,"* (1 John 4:4); *"I can do all things through Christ which* strengtheneth me," (*Philippians 4:13*); "*I am crucified with Christ: nevertheless I live; yet not I, but Christ liveth in me: and the life which I now live in the flesh I live by the faith of the Son of God, who loved me, and gave himself for me,*" (*Galatians 2:20*)."

With that, I picked up my lawn chair and Bible and plowed through the tall grass fearlessly and courageously. When I was back in the house I knew things were not the same and never would be outside. But that was okay because I was not ever going to be the same either. **Sure, I knew what it was to be abandoned, but more importantly: I knew that Jesus … would never abandon me!**

My focus was on Jesus. We walked through the house together in harmony. He did not yell at me or torment me or try to intimidate me, let alone threaten me or hurt me. Jesus was so peaceful and loving and stable and solid and trustworthy. I was not afraid of Jesus. I knew I could trust Him to treat me right, like a lady. It was wonderful the way He reassured me of His presence.

That is not something that is easy to explain. I just knew that I knew deep inside that I was not alone. There was nothing spooky about it; I just knew that my Savior was with me. The more you get to know Jesus—and you do so by spending time with Him—the more easily and quickly you sense His presence. You cannot spend time in the presence of the Lord and not be changed.

He just fills you with everything positive like life and love and joy and peace. Even if you don't have any problems, when you become aware of being in His presence you will still come away changed for the better. The peace that passes all understanding (*Philippians 4:7*) is something that money cannot buy, and it cannot be counterfeited by the devil. It pays fantastic dividends to spend time with Jesus. You will never have to fear abandonment. **Faith… knows He is faithful. It is that simple.**

God's ways are higher than our ways, (*Isaiah 55:9*). He can use a simple incident to trigger a volcanic eruption of healing, even in the heart of someone who has been harboring ill will. I know, because I did not always want to forgive, let alone feel like forgiving. Sometimes the stress got to me and I reacted with retaliation. Every pressure cooker has a valve for a reason ... repent, get the release, or the situation worsens, gradually making it dangerous for all.

So I repented and got a release, although not all of the hurt was gone. Some hurts are far deeper than others and require a lot of love to replace the pain. God replaced the pain with His love each time that I was able to receive. I had to learn to trust God more, and He knew it. He knew my faith was sorely damaged, though I did believe for restoration. **He was healing me His way ... from the inside out! God is thorough!** He is absolutely awesome. "*...with God all things are possible,*" (*Matthew 19:26*).

I can only encourage you to hold tightly to Jesus, because when you determine to keep your heart right with Him, He will see you through anything! There will be no limits. He makes a way where there is no way (*Isaiah 43:19*). He will go before you (*Luke 7:27*). Stay focused because Jesus said, "*... I am the way, the truth, and the life: no man cometh unto the Father, but by me,*" (*John 14:6*).

# 42. PAINFUL REALITY

I HURT, A LOT. MUCH AS I tried to, I did not walk in the Spirit all of the time. There were times when I battled discouragement, questions about the future, family, job, finances, housing, friends, and my marital status, not to mention the natural aging process.

Not everyone talks about it, but a lot of people sure do a lot of things to help prevent themselves from appearing older. They try make-up, working out, a new hair color, a toupee, a wig—whatever it takes. I found my mind thinking about my age, size, wrinkles, image—and even though I knew who I was in Christ, and that I was fearfully and wonderfully made (*Psalm 139:14*), I wanted to do better with my physical appearance.

When a person believes he/she looks good, that person walks differently. There is a confidence exuded from within. It could be a simple thing such as a flattering new hair style, yet the new image results in a new lilt to the step, a bounce in his/her walk.

So where did that leave me? Facing facts, as I sat on the glider swing that I had moved into our large living room. Most of the furniture was in storage. The swing was a comfortable place to sit as I prepared to watch a detective movie. I knew I should read the Word or pray or praise the Lord, but my heart was finding it difficult to get spiritual. Not that it is not spiritual to watch a movie, but I knew at that time it was not what I was to be doing.

Just before the movie began, I sat and swung gently, trying to just listen to the Lord. Tears filled my eyes and my heart hurt as the grief spilled out. I did not want to hurt. I wanted to be brave, courageous and strong in the Lord, yet when everything was quiet, the hurt came out. As I brushed away the tears of sorrow, loneliness, heartbreak, rejection and pain, the Lord spoke to me so gently and softly. He said, *"It will be over soon."*

More tears fell. The love that Jesus released to my heart was so tender and wonderful I couldn't help but cry. He is so faithful to encourage just when it is most needed. You see, I had come home from church and spent the afternoon eating lunch alone, then I had a nap. After that, a friend called and I shared the morning's sermon with her. Everyone else was busy doing their own thing, and I fully intended to study or pray, but I did neither.

Instead, I found myself spending quiet time in the secret place—the place where I met with God regularly to commune, pray, listen, learn, receive and worship, although my secret place moved to the swing. That was okay though, because I found out Jesus liked to sit on the swing with me and relax too. His words told me that He was fully aware of the difficulties I was facing. I was not looking for sympathy, but it was hard when all I had for the offering at church that morning was two quarters.

I had tried not to cry because it was so little, yet when I filled out my receipt the Lord honored my honesty and humility. He knew others would read that fifty cent receipt and have their own thoughts about it, but He also knew my heart. I was glad, because that was all that mattered.

Jesus knew it was all I had, except for the thirty-five cents at home that I saved for the next meeting on Wednesday. God always honors obedience, so I sowed the money. Then why did I hurt when I was just being obedient?

I did not understand until after I put my offering in the envelope. My spirit did not get a witness as that envelope travelled down the aisle so I bowed my head and prayed, *"Father, what is wrong?"*

He told me right away. The truth hurt too. He said, *"You did not trust Me completely; you put your trust in that credit card this week and now this is your offering to Me. I want you to trust Me completely."* I knew immediately what He was talking about. I had been expecting some money that was due me but it had not arrived yet. Rather than trust God and wait for His provision, I had used my credit card.

I sucked in my breath and repented immediately, *"Father, I am so sorry, please forgive me for running out of patience. I repent. I am so sorry I hurt you Father. Please forgive me, in Jesus' Name."* Then I stood on the Word in *1 John 1:9* that says, *"If we confess our sins, he is faithful and just to forgive us our sins, and to cleanse us from all unrighteousness,"* and I thanked my Heavenly Father.

I sighed. I wanted to kick my own butt, yet condemnation is not from God so I made a quick decision not to look back, but not to repeat what I did either. I cut up the credit card.

Here's what had happened: I had bought a bottle of my favorite cologne because I had not had any for months. I had been praying the Lord would put it on someone's heart to purchase the cologne for me, but that did not happen. I thought that I had been patient in waiting so long, and since I was expecting a check to arrive in a few days, I made the purchase when I had a ride to the store.

God's viewpoint was different though. He also saw me do the same thing when I ordered a new supply of skin cream and vitamins online. Even though I was going to pay the bill as soon as the check arrived, which indicated my intentions were good, it was not the right thing to do from God's perspective. His ways are higher. He was teaching me to trust Him.

Really, can you see Jesus using a credit card? Can you picture Him getting too impatient to wait for a check that had been held up in the mail? Can you see Him just whipping out the plastic and taking care of business? Nope. Absolutely not. Now, do not misunderstand what I am saying here. It is NOT a sin to use a credit card when you can pay it off each month. In my situation, though, even though I intended to pay it off, it was wrong for me because it was temptation and I had a way out. I could have waited.

God deals with each of us individually, so in this kind of situation what was wrong for me may not be wrong for you, and vice versa. I knew I was never to compromise. To do so once I learned the will of God for me was very wrong, and this was what had happened in this situation. The bottom line was that I did not prioritize properly. The scripture says to put God first (*Matthew 6:33*). Instead, I put my needs first.

Just when I got one situation cleared up and started to feel better about myself because I knew I was maturing and learning God's ways, I faced some adversity in another area.

After church I faced strong confusion as I looked at the disarray that moving brought to the house. I was used to keeping an orderly house, and this was stressful. I was also resisting painful memories as I kept finding certain photos of the past. It was good that God was pulling out the hurts, yet it was painful. It would have been easy to phone someone and ask them to come over for a visit, but I knew God was not telling me to do that.

He wanted me to lean on Him, not on other people. Besides, people had shown me how little time they had for me. There were very few who offered to help me pack or transport anything, yet many knew I was on my own and making a major move.

This taught me to keep my eyes on Jesus. It took nearly six weeks to complete the move because only one couple could come for three hours a week. A few others used their cars to pick up a load from time to time. It was a long, drawn out affair. At times I had to battle anger because my husband didn't help me at all with the work of moving.

Thinking back to a previous move, I remembered that Clint did not help when we sold our single-wide mobile home and bought the new double-wide. Remembering this pulled me out of more denial. It forced me to see that he had not been around to help when we moved into the first home, or out of it to the double-wide. He simply did not want to help me.

I remembered that when we were thinking about buying the larger mobile home, we went to our pastor for counseling. Clint had said that if our pastor said anything against buying the home, he would not buy it. If Pastor said it was all right, he would buy it. I agreed and left it in God's hands, but

I knew what the outcome would be. I had received a vision from the Lord a year earlier.

It was a vision of a double-wide mobile home, and I had spent months viewing new models and doing my homework. I studied floor plans and kept looking until this new model arrived. As soon as I went inside I knew it was the one. Clint would not go even ten miles to see it so I took pictures and he looked at them. I had heard from God and would not be discouraged. **I talked a lot more with the Lord than with my husband.**

Clint signed on the dotted line, and it did not take long to know he did so begrudgingly. When it was delivered he refused to move even one item. He took great delight in such manipulation, and with smugness he visited others while I moved. He enjoyed sinking his toes in the plush carpet though, and he enjoyed the fireplace in the winter. Texas does have snow and does have winter.

So now that I was moving again I was reliving all of this. I was no longer in denial. I accepted the fact that he did not support me in so many ways as he should have. I had made our house a home with God's help, but the massive volume of heartache in my marriage helped me let go of our home now. God had given me the grace and strength I needed then, and He was giving it to me again in this situation. I was being reminded Who my Source was.

I received persecution, yes, but great rewards too because nothing is hid from the Lord (*Matthew 10:26*). For me, delivery day of the double-wide mobile home was fulfillment of the vision that I received from the Lord, and I proclaimed it. It was also restoration because I had been robbed of a beautiful home years before I had allowed Jesus to be Lord of my life. God knew it. He doesn't change (*Malachi 3:6*), so I had hope that He had a home all picked out for me and I would live there in His timing. Restoration is a good thing. Restoration is a God thing. "...*he restoreth my soul.*" (*Psalm 23:3*). "*Restore unto me the joy of thy salvation;*" (*Psalm 51:12*). "*For I will restore health unto thee, and heal thee of thy wounds saith the LORD;*" (*Jeremiah 30:17*).

# 43. SCATTERBRAIN

SOMETIMES I FEEL LIKE A SCATTERBRAIN, but that doesn't mean I am. That was what I was thinking about at the end of a not very happy evening. The Spirit of God prompted me to write about what I was experiencing, and I obeyed. My purpose is to let you know that I am most certainly human and experience the same attacks of fear, insecurity, and other negative emotions that others experience. How we handle the attacks is what may differ.

That morning my pastor taught on 'Resistance'. It was a timely message for me. So too was his mention of the fiery furnace and the four men IN the furnace. The teaching helped me to view my situation with spiritually opened eyes. There is much going on in the spirit realm. I needed to be more diligent regarding spiritual warfare.

The pastor stated that we must change our position, rise, and resist the enemy—resist all darkness. When we are in position we will be resisting darkness, not tolerating darkness. The church will be powerless when there is no resistance to darkness. Everyone wants the glory but few want to experience the furnace. The greater the resistance, the greater the power and the glory. No compromise.

I meditated on these thoughts and waited on the Lord. Well, if the credit card deal and the resistance were not enough spiritual steak to chew on for a few days, up came another nugget. The pastor had said, *"The Lord told you before to get off caffeine."* I sat there and knew it was true. I was still drinking my favorite soda. It was of some consolation to know God had set me free from the bondage of having to have coffee, so at least I knew I was making headway.

Yes, I always check my own heart when I hear a sermon. I don't wonder about the people next to or in front of me. When I go to church I expect to hear from the Lord and I do. I may not always like what I hear, but I know God is in the changing business. He knows how to let me know what changes He wants to bring forth in my life.

There is always a purpose in the changes He brings because He does not do anything without a purpose, so I know any suffering I go through will not be in vain. In the long run I will be glad I submitted to God, resisted the devil, and chose to crucify the flesh. In doing so I become a light that shines brighter and brighter and brighter as God fills me with His power and His glory. He can do it if I resist the darkness and trust Him completely.

Since my trust in man was broken, God knew how much it meant for my trust in Him to remain intact. He knew my experiences in the natural could have a tendency to spill over and affect my trust in Him. He was being very loving and patient with me, for which I was so thankful. I had said to a friend of mine, when we were talking about my situation, *"If you can't trust your husband, who can you trust?"* There was no reply. Later the Lord reminded me of what I said and He told me, *"You can trust Me."*

Now, that amazed me. Those four little words meant so much and I knew they were absolutely true. Jesus never lets anyone down, and He never breaks a promise. We need to keep our part of the promise, and He will keep His. He is awesome.

Well, this and the previous chapter are somewhat somber and sobering, yet enlightening. I pray they are beneficial to each of my readers. The chapters, and the experiences that inspired them, do not bring a big smile to my face, but as I read them I have peace in my heart. I sense the wonderful presence of the Lord and know that my Shepherd will lead me through the valley.

It is a journey guaranteed to be full of challenges, changes, and choices— all of which I pray that I accept and am successful in to the end. **I do not think Job smiled every day; yet his life brought much glory to God. That is what it is all about. I want my life to bring glory to God, and I pray that is your prayer for your life too.**

# 44. DEAD END OR DETOUR?

If I look at circumstances in my life right now
It is a dead end I see
Most definitely
Why
Because my husband left me
Took my name off the bank accounts
Changed the pin number
Cancelled two months' mortgage payments
Quit paying on the land
I have no job
My car was repossessed
He is threatening to force foreclosure
On our home and the land
I put the furniture in storage

Then I moved in with a Christian family
Three days ago
God gave me favor
The wife came to me at church
Her husband told her they have the extra bedroom
If I need it, it is okay with him
I cried and felt such a huge burden lift off my shoulders
A certain phase of my life was left behind at that moment
God had gone before me and prepared the way
I had only met this family weeks before
When they offered me a ride to church regularly

They have four children yet made time for me
In the hot Texas sun this woman and I moved box after box
In her Jeep Cherokee that was such a blessing indeed
She was exhausted too but we got it done
The Lord led me to a couple that knew the pain of divorce
Talk about going through a shaking
I had five dollars in my wallet
Eight dollars in the bank account
And that is it
But all of the above
Are just circumstances
It is most necessary to see spiritually
What is happening
God's viewpoint differs greatly from mine

God sees when I pray, obey, stand on the Word
Yet the ship crashes, so to speak
God sees when I lean on Him
And when I do things as unto Him
Yet when the bottom fell out
It hurt my faith

So what do I do

How do I keep from feeling
Like the Lord let me down
Because deep in my heart
I know He didn't
I must stay in the Word
To keep my chin up

Never stop trusting God
Rejoice in the Lord always (*Philippians 4:4*)
What more can I say
Except that it is exactly two years
Since I moved into this home
I remember because it is my son's birthday

*Note: The following poem was written for a friend whose home I lived in for several months after the separation.*

# 45. HAPPY FATHER'S DAY

Some men don't like fussin'
And all that kind of stuff
But you deserve to be honored
Sure 'nuff

I've seen you wearing the hat
Of a father, a husband, a friend
So though I've known you a short time
Knew a poem I should send

Sometimes the viewpoint of others
Is different than what self sees
So in case this is true
Here is how it bees☺

You love your family
That is obvious to anyone
You work from the heart
So a good job is done

Your brain works on the opposite side
Of your wife's
And will do so
The rest of your life

That is good though
God keeps balance for all

So continue to press on
As you answer His call

His plan for you is good
He will make each phase clear
The steps of a righteous man
Are ordered by the Lord *(Psalm 37:23)*
He is always near

So do not worry at all
Trust Him to lead you day by day
When your eyes are on Jesus
Your heart will not go astray

Just for the record I want to say
Thank you for blessing me
When I had great need
I pray God blesses you accordingly

It is good fruit in your life
And that of your family
When you are willing to share
Such wonderful hospitality

Words can't express
How y'all have blessed me
Suffice to say
Immensely

So have a Happy Father's Day
Though you aren't my dad
But if you were
I'd have to say I'm glad

If your kids read this poem
I bet they would agree
Your wife too
So, enjoy life and BE HAPPY

This is a poem I wrote for the man of the house that became my home for four months. When I moved out of my home, he and his wife and children welcomed me. They became an extension of Jesus Christ as they opened not only their door, but their hearts to me. To be on the receiving end of such openness and sincerity was humbling. With four children, not to mention farm animals that needed feeding too, their home was a busy place!

At the time, there were additional children and two adult men sleeping here. The men were truck drivers who had their children with them because school was out. This home had an open door because the host and hostess had open hearts. The only problem was the meals: brisket, baked beans, potato salad … well you get the picture. The hostess was an excellent cook and enjoyed cooking for others. Praise the Lord!

No doubt if it was Jesus who needed a roof over His head, He would be well received in this home. Or if He needed to freshen up with a shower and a shave and eat a good meal, as did the truckers and their families, He would receive just what He needed.

Does your home have an open door? Would you have to have everything spic and span before inviting someone over? Would you invite them to see everything but not even offer them a beverage or a seat? What kind of servant are you? Jesus is our example. That is just a little food for thought. Hmm.

From my experience this couple was one in a million in how they used their home for the glory of God. It was healing for me just in how they welcomed me with no strings attached. They did not expect me to become the cleaning lady or the cook. Nor did they insist I apply for social assistance so I could help them financially. They just wanted me to rest and recover. It was overwhelming. They honored me. God was so faithful to put people like this in my path.

Incidentally, when I left their home to move on, I told them I did not know how, but I knew God would bless them in such a way that they would know for sure He did it. He did. **They received a $10,000 cash gift, totally unexpectedly, just a couple of weeks after I moved out. Glory to God. When you do what you do as unto the Lord Jesus Christ, He will not be indebted to you; He will repay. His dividends are always impressive. This couple solved a problem for me and God solved a problem for them.**

# 46.  HOME SWEET HOME

When I hear the word

H - O - M - E

My mind draws a blank

Empty; nothing comes to mind

No frame, no particular style or color

Nothing

When it comes to identifying

With home

There is nothing there to identify with.

Home is gone

Home is no more

Home is not

Home

Less

I am homeless


But when I study the Bible

I learn God knows what I need

God does not change

God still performs miracles

God's Word will not come back void

It will accomplish what it is sent to do

I say what God says

When I can't; God can

It is the people who live by faith

Who are the true sons of Abraham

It is a spiritual battle
So I take authority spiritually
I rebuke every ungodly, unedifying
Word or thought that comes against me
And pull down those strongholds
In the Name of Jesus

God vindicates me
God provides seed
I sowed in good soil
I bear testimony
God gives me a mouth and such utterance
And wisdom that all my foes
Combined will be unable to stand

I gave
I receive
With God nothing is impossible
Ask, Seek, Knock
The door will be opened to you
Windows of Heaven are open
When I become a giver
I automatically move myself
Into the realm of a receiver
Exceedingly abundantly above
The wealth of the sinner
Is laid up for the just
The peace of God rules in my heart
No good thing will he withhold

*(Galatians 3:7; 2 Corinthians 10:3-5; Matthew 10:7-20; 2 Corinthians 9:10; Luke 21:13-15; Luke 6:38; Luke 1:37; Matthew 7:7; Matthew 6:33; Malachi 3:10; Ephesians 3:10; Proverbs 13:22; Colossians 3:15; Psalms 84:11)*

**Bottom line: I was encouraging myself in the Lord.**

# 47. HIS ADDICTIVE PRESENCE

I'm so glad the presence of the Lord
Is extremely addictive
I choose to be addicted to Him
A person addicted to drugs, tobacco, alcohol
Cannot go without such vices
That is why I choose to be
Addicted to Jesus
Because He can be trusted

Even when we can't predict the outcome
I do not ever want to be without Him
I can do nothing without Him
With God, all things are possible
To him who believes (*Mark 9:23*)
And I do

What you are addicted to
Becomes a part of you
The two become one
You cannot do without the other
You become a team

It becomes common knowledge
That it is no longer just 'you'
Your identity is marked
By what or to whom you are addicted
The fruit your life produces

Is the evidence of your addiction
You have a serious addiction
He is serious about you too
Check the fruit in your life
Are you, **"Addicted to Jesus?"**

# 48. KNOCK, KNOCK

BECAUSE I AM ADDICTED TO JESUS, He had already prepared me for the next surprise. Not all surprises are good, so I was thankful for the advance preparation. When I walked to the car to go to the post office, a sixteen-year-old girl asked me if she could drive. I agreed to be the licensed passenger, as this made it legal for her to drive with a beginner's permit.

As we approached the car I asked her if she had her permit with her since all I saw was a key chain and a small change purse in her hand. She responded, "Oh, I don't have a permit."

I stopped in my tracks with a definite check in my spirit. (Meaning it was like a red light on the inside, a warning, the equivalent of a red flag.) As I looked up to the sky I said, *"Oh Lord, here we go again. Help me be bold and take a stand for righteousness' sake."*

I said, *"You don't? I did not know that. I thought you had a permit."* She explained that she had started taking a drivers' education course, but her father (with whom she was living at the time) made her quit. I said, *"I can't go if you don't have a permit. That is against the law."* Her sister, who was on the front lawn drinking iced tea, laughed so hard she spit out her tea.

I continued, *"I have learned to submit to the law of the land so I cannot do this. If we are stopped, do you know what could happen?"* She said she would not be able to drive until she was eighteen years of age. Then she told me she had twenty dollars and she would give it to me in case of a fine. I said, *"I answer to God and to blatantly do this would be to disobey Him. I made a decision not to compromise a long time ago."* The girls retreated to the house.

I sat on the swing and prayed for the parents who were in the house, that they would use godly wisdom, and that they would not give me a hard time for speaking up. Soon one of the girls came out and handed me the keys so I could go get the mail, but she would not be going. She said her dad told her that if I was not comfortable then let me drive. I drove. When I returned, nothing was said about the incident.

I was seeing opportunity for decisions to be made in the arenas of obedience versus disobedience, and rebellion against authority or submission. God uses people to expose darkness, but He will not force people to obey. A police officer is a minister of God. When it comes to exposing darkness, can God use you? Has He been knocking on your heart's door? Have you been nudged to speak up? Is there fear of man and man's rejection? Do you fear God more? Could it be He is knocking, right now?

# 49. FRIENDS?

I called a new friend
She returned my call thirty hours later
The same thing happened
A second time
She stated that she can't be on the phone
Every day
She never did find out
Why I called

I called another friend
She listened as I shared good news
But she did not respond
The conversation was strained
I did not know if she did not hear
Or if she did without responding

I asked her if she went to sleep
After pausing
And still no response
She said, *"No, I'm listening."*
You can tell if you have
Someone's undivided attention or not
Listening to someone on the phone
Who is simultaneously watching TV
Tends to hinder
What could have been
A blessed time of fellowship

Consequently, I decided
Not to waste time on the phone
Rather, I will be more focused on the Lord
Guess what happened
I was praying today
And watching tennis championships on TV
At the same time

So my own poem
Resulted in my being convicted
That's good though
Because I want to be more Christ-like
And I can't picture Jesus
Praying to the Father
While watching TV simultaneously

I do know I am praying
That God chooses my friends for me
Male and female
Because I do not want to be pulled down
By people whose phone
Is used as a weapon
Rather than as a tool to serve them

In fact, I choose to guard
The anointing God has given me
And I want even more
A greater anointing

It is a new beginning in my life
Much more than a new chapter though
I do not want "hit and run" friends
People who want to know your business
But won't come and visit
Won't take you out somewhere
When you don't have a car
Even if it is just to the park
To enjoy the outdoors

Inhospitable Christians
Do not impress me at all
I see it all the time
Thank God for those I do know
Who have an open heart
And an open home too

Thank God HE is always there
Without Him
I don't know what I would do
Suffice to say
**"What kind of a friend are you?"**

# 50. TRANSITION

I see land Lord
What does this mean
Jesus and I stepped forward
Making the transition
From walking on the water
To walking on a beach and land

I still have not swum
In the natural that is
But I sure walked on the water
And danced and danced on the water
With Jesus
It was wonderful

But now I enter a new beginning
As life goes on
Feet on solid ground
Sounds like a less stressful time
Or at least my faith is not being tried as severely

You are not leaving me though Lord
You'll be with me
Whether we are walking on water, on ground, in fire
Thank you Lord for never leaving me
Also, I thank you for revealing
That before I reached land
I was cleansed, purified and fitted for service

In the Kingdom of God
I am reminded of a prophecy given to me recently
*"You are to rest for a while*
*Then I will have something for you to do."*

# 51. JESUS WON'T LET ME DOWN

He reminded me of the vision I wrote about earlier
Jesus carried my husband away from me
I pulled my husband safely to shore
Then I stood up to get my breath and my footing
When I looked up I saw Jesus walking away from me
Across the sand carrying my husband in his arms like a baby
Then Jesus called me to walk on the water

Not alone, with Jesus
I stand there now
Feeling the water under my feet
Ripples, current drawing me downward
Yet peace in my heart and stability
Waves larger at times
Yet no fear
Assurance that all is well

I stand secure in Christ
He does not expect me to sink
I won't let Him down
Because I know He won't let me down
We are a team
Christ in me
The hope of glory (*Colossians 1:27*)

*Note: I am simply sharing my thoughts during a season of R&R*
*(Rest and Recuperation)*

# 52. JUST BEING HONEST

BEING TRANSPARENT IS NOT EASY, BUT it is necessary. It means I must step out of the way and let God be God whether I like what He is doing or not. Otherwise my book would be written in vain. The Lord knows how to motivate me.

I was sitting in my room, thinking about the upcoming church barbeque for the 40-60 year old singles. My stomach almost churned when I thought about it, yet I knew the Lord was nudging me to go. My heart told me it was really no big deal—just get together for a chance to fellowship as well as to enjoy a meal with other believers. My head was saying something different.

I realized I was starved for fellowship and contact with friends, yet I was right where God wanted me to be. So I had drawn closer to the Lord and had complete assurance of His nearness and ability to fill every void, yet there was something else that concerned me.

What if I did meet someone, a man, who was easy to talk to and wanted to talk to me? I did not need any temptation, did not want any, and would rather stay home than risk running head on into temptation. Why? Because my heart was heavy. I felt sad, rejected, betrayed and abandoned, so going out was just not on my agenda. I preferred to stay home and read a good book or do some writing. So why did the Lord want me to go to this dinner?

I knew I would not know why He wanted me to go until I went. I knew He had a plan and I knew I needed to obey, but that did not mean my head and my heart were in agreement at that moment. I just hoped they would be by the time Thursday—the day of the barbeque—rolled around. I felt like I was making a mountain out of a molehill, but that was how things were at that time. I needed healing. I needed reassurance of my attractiveness as a woman, my desirability as a woman, my intelligence. *"God, why does life have to be so complicated?"*

I was fully aware that some people in my situation would just put on a pair of jeans or shorts, get ready and go. Well, me being me, meant that I had to face some fear. So what was I afraid of? Man. Men. How was I going to overcome that fear? Face it; just face the fear and not run. I had to deal with my feelings, not stay in denial, and not let fear overcome me.

Just thinking about going was upsetting me. I did not want to be bothered by any single men, because for sure I was not looking for a man, and I knew word was out that I was separated. I had enough to think about and contend with already.

Undoubtedly there were men who had been hurt too and would not want to go to a social function any more than I did. However, just because I could empathize with them did not mean I was ready to do anything about anything. In fact, I really just wanted to sit on the fence and do nothing. Just dig my heels in a bit.

But where would that get me? Stuck. That's all. Stuck. No, worse than that because I'd be sliding downward. There is no such thing as a neutral position spiritually. No such thing as effective fence sitting. It is backsliding and I was not fixin' to go there. I was determined to climb upward, pressing in.

Suddenly everything seemed so wrong. My hair needed to be trimmed; it needed a body perm; my nails needed to be done; I needed a tan—I was finding it all too easy to attack myself, and it didn't do much except to make me feel anything but good about myself.

I thought back to my marriage and remembered when I looked after myself and got criticized for wearing makeup and a skirt or dress first thing in the morning, even though I wasn't going to work. I did it for Clint, but what good did it do? He was unfaithful.

So I decided that if I was going to look after myself, it was not going to be to keep a man; it was not going to be to impress someone. No, I would look after myself and keep myself attractive for myself, because it makes me feel good about myself. It helps my own self esteem. Men aren't the only ones that have an ego.

I determined to look after myself because I am an ambassador for Christ, and as His representative I want to know I have put forth my best, whether it is my best attitude, best appearance, or whatever. I decided that I was here to bring glory to God. That was what was important. **Besides, Jesus goes with me everywhere I go, so why not fix myself up as if I had a date with Him that will never end!! It will never be finished. Praise the Lord. What better reason could anyone have to fix up than because of having a date with none other than Jesus?!!!**

Okay, I bared my heart—the fear, hurts, doubts, junk in general. I decided I would rise above all the junk, though, because I chose to be "... *more than a conqueror in Christ Jesus...*" (*Romans 8:37*). It was a decision I was able to make with the help of the Lord. Whether it was hot or cold out, rainy or sunny, I chose to rejoice in the Lord; to be thankful that this is the day that the Lord has made (*Psalms 118:24*).

I also chose to encourage myself in the Lord, and for sure not to wait for someone else to encourage me. I determined not to look to any man or woman to do so. That much I did learn a long time ago. People will let me down, but Jesus will never let me down. So what was I stewing about? I needed to change my focus from self and self-centeredness to Jesus. Christ-centeredness was and still is my choice.

You see, I am human too, not yet perfected, but I am on my way. I choose to climb up, climb up higher. No mountain is too tall to climb. With God all things are possible (*Matthew 19:26*). I just pray He reveals more of His plan for my life, because where there is no vision the people perish (*Proverbs 29:18*). Everyone needs to see a light at the end of the tunnel.

# 53. TO LAUGH AGAIN

It is so wonderful
To laugh again
I had forgotten
How great it is
To have a good laugh
Even greater
To have more than one good laugh
... in the same day ...
Let alone the same hour

In fact, it felt so wonderful
I made a quality decision
Laughter must be a part of my life
Each and every day
A merry heart does good like a medicine (*Proverbs 17:22*).
I like having a merry heart
I like laughing
I like its infectious effect on others
I believe it is quite all right with God too

Come to think of it
I know a lot of people
Who would benefit equally as much as I do
If they enjoyed a good laugh regularly too
So after writing this little gem

I can hardly wait
To see God's plan for tomorrow
For me, and for others too
Yahooooooooooooooooo!

# 54. STAY COOL

I WAS THINKING BACK TO THE day when I went to see a lawyer. I did not go alone. God is my attorney and He went with me to that office. God took my case, but the attorney wouldn't. He wanted cash and I didn't have any. Money talks. I understood. So, I was NOT able to file for divorce as I had intended.

It seemed my hands were tied, so to speak, and the door was not open. At first I kind of felt like I had hit the wall, yet I had peace. (The flesh dies hard; it can't be cast out, it must be crucified, daily.) The Lord spoke only two words to me: *"Don't fight."* It was as simple as that. A huge wave of His peace that passes all understanding *(Philippians 4:7)* hit me, bathing me completely. I did not fight. I let go of everything and put my trust in Him. He is my Source anyway.

It was of some consolation knowing the lawyer had agreed to mail a letter to my husband in an attempt to get some communication started. That letter was sent at no cost to me. God gave me favor with man. My money speaks more loudly because I return the first ten percent (the tithe) to God, and that breaks a curse off my money. The ninety percent left is blessed *(Malachi 3:9-11)*. Also, I give offerings above that amount and am promised God will always give back to me more *(Luke 6:38)*.

When an attorney sends a letter without charging, that is favor with man. Little is much when God is in it, and I had not turned my face away from Him.

God sees the big picture. Little did I know He had a purpose in that letter being sent. He was fixin' to expose some darkness. The Lord wanted me to know what was going on elsewhere while I was waiting a whole two months for the attorney to mail the letter.

Consequently, I was beginning to feel like the persistent widow in the Bible that finally received favor from the judge *(Mark 7:28)*. My phone calls asking for the letter (even though I was not being charged for the letter to be written) became more frequent. I was holding the lawyer to his word. He and I had a verbal agreement. It took two months, but he kept his word, thank God; and with God's help I managed to keep my cool. Through tribulation one becomes more patient; I'm sort of hoping my cup is full of patience!

Please, get this. What looked like a closed door, according to the circumstances, was not. Faith is not something one sees ... or it wouldn't be faith. My faith was being tried, big time. Texas was hot and so was the furnace. Only God could provide central air in the midst of it all, and He did!

What did I do? I went home and offered a sacrifice of praise to the Lord (*Hebrews 13:15*) because by faith I believed that He was fighting the battles for me. *Psalm 46:10* told me to be still and know that He is God. To be still also meant to cease striving. That took some time, but it happened. My faith and trust stayed in the Lord, my Lord.

What did my husband do during that time? Eleven days earlier he filed for a divorce. Several weeks had passed and I had not been served with any papers, so I did not know he had filed. If that blessed letter had not been sent by my lawyer ... I would have been divorced without knowing it. Nor would I have had an opportunity to contest anything. Sneaky, but that was okay.

**God reveals the strategies of my enemies and it did not cost me a thing to learn the truth.** My husband phoned the lawyer to let him know he had already filed for a divorce in July.

My lawyer called me with the good news. I saw pieces of the puzzle coming together bit by bit. I was not served with a petition for divorce because my husband stated that he did not know where I lived. (He frequently attended my home church, and I lived less than a mile from our home at the time.) It was necessary for him to have the petition for divorce posted on the board at the courthouse.

My husband filed for the divorce. Eleven days later I saw a lawyer who did not write a letter for me until two months later. That is how we discovered my husband had already filed. God would not let me file. Darkness had to leave. God's hand was on the whole situation. I was learning much about the timing of God and in being led by the Holy Spirit.

The patience of God wears out the devil. Please understand, I am not calling anyone the devil. It was a spiritual battle. I do not hate men or any man. I forgave and I continue to forgive. It was a process. It was because I kept my eyes on Jesus that I am not like a lot of people who are divorced and bitter.

They are still unhappy though they are single again! Divorce does not make anyone happy. If all it took to be happy was a divorce, everyone would be divorced and happy, but that is not so. Heart condition is paramount. Divorce is a result of hardened hearts, but hearts do not have to stay hard.

Divorce is a provision for hardened hearts (*Matthew 19:8*). I had not hardened my heart, so it would have been wrong for me to get a divorce (please understand, that does not mean it is wrong to divorce if someone is in a life-threatening situation). Judgment fell on my husband and I was released from the marriage. He left me. He divorced me. Light does not leave. Darkness leaves. That is what the Lord told me, and I saw it manifested when the divorce was final.

God revealed through my life, experientially, how severe the spiritual battle had been. He also revealed that He was (and is!) in control, not man and not the evil forces that try to influence man. There are no coincidences. The hand of God is always at work and is not to be overlooked. He is always working on behalf of His children; His children just need to recognize and cooperate with Him.

God has a purpose in all that He does. Christians need to recognize the work of the enemy, spiritually, and take authority over the darkness. God was able to work on my behalf because I spoke the Word of God … believed the Word of God … and my faith was in God.

It does not mean that we will not suffer. It means that we will be able to comfort and help others because of the help we received from the Lord in our own personal Gethsemane: *"Who comforteth us in all our tribulation that we may be able to comfort them which are in any trouble, by the comfort wherewith we ourselves are comforted of God,"* (2 Corinthians 1:4).

He becomes our hand extended, as am I to you through this book. Open your heart and let that hurt out. Apply the blood of Jesus and the washing of the Word. Replace the pain with truth and healing as Jesus walks into the dark areas with you. He wants to make you whole, nothing broken, and He is able. He did it for me and He does not love me more than anyone else; or any less for that matter.

I know God hates abuse, and both men and women have suffered from abuse. It does not have to stay that way. It is time to take a stand against it, come out of denial and get out of the closet of shame and regret. Stand up, pull your shoulders back and use the authority you have been given in the Name of Jesus. It matters not what you lose materially, financially, etc. Fifty years from now those things won't matter anyway.

God is in the restoration business and He does not change. Even if you end up like I did, with three pieces of luggage when I returned to Canada and a broken, shattered heart, I still had Jesus. And when you have Jesus, you have all you need. He RESTORES, to the glory of God. Check it out in the Bible. Don't spend a lot of time with people who cannot help you. Choose your friends carefully.

Spend time with the Master Potter and He will do more for you in five minutes than any person can in ten years. That is the way God is. He knows better than anyone what you need and how to help you. Who knows better than our Creator how to fix us? If your car breaks down, do you take it to the dentist? Same difference. Well, sort of. I trust you get the picture. Jesus is the answer, no matter what the problem.

**He wants me to share how He makes Himself real to me whether it is through a book, a song, a poem, etc. That is what this book is all about.** I live it first, then I write about it. I am not feeding off someone else's testimony, like a vulture. This eagle has been soaring for some time and is fixin' to soar even higher. God is graciously working it all together for good as only He can, according to *Romans 8:28.*

**If you won't spend time in God's Word getting to know Him, don't expect to recognize His voice or have enough strength and power to soar.** Just remember, if you choose to be like a chicken in the barnyard with someone else always feeding you, your days will be numbered with little opportunity to glorify God, cooped up (pardon the pun) in the chicken coop.

A flying chicken is not very stable and is actually a threat to other chickens in the barnyard, especially when landing. Where would you like to be? Ducking a flying chicken or soaring like an eagle toward the heavenlies? God leaves the decision to you.

Let's look at some other circumstances too. Even with all of the adverse circumstances I have faced, I do not have headaches. I am not depressed. I am not suicidal. I still hear from God. I do not have to go see a counselor or cry to the pastor, or anyone else for that matter, because there is nothing to cry about!

When I look at this situation spiritually I see darkness—the evil deeds that came against me big time—being pushed AWAY from me. Instead of a mountain of adversity overcoming me, God turned the stumbling blocks into stepping stones. He put steps on the mountain as I dealt with each problem, with His help, until I reached the top of the mountain—a very high mountain, because the valley was very, very, low!

I am a candidate for restoration. The devil has to restore sevenfold all he has taken from me according to *Proverbs 6:31.* Plus. I believe God's promises in *Joel 2:23,24,* so **restoration is not an option. Restoration is a promise, and God honors His Word.**

*Hebrews 11:6* tells me God is a rewarder of those that diligently seek Him, and I do. I don't do anything without Him. I have increased faith. I soar as an eagle because I feed on live food, the Word of God. That is why I have the strength to persevere and can be a forerunner breaking through the darkness. There is no fear. *2 Timothy 1:7* tells me I have not been given the spirit of fear but of power, love, and a sound mind. I have the mind of Christ and I use it according to *Philippians 2:5.* **Bottom line: The Word Works!**

The Word of God does not work only for the dynamic preachers I have listened to often on Christian television. The Word works for me just as effectively. It is because of God's Word and faithfulness that I can stand. I am not on the floor of the boxing ring. I have my arms upraised, giving glory to God. **It is a knockout for me because the enemy had to release his hold. Get that!!!! The devil is defeated! Strongholds have been broken by the power of God!!**

When God's judgment fell because of my husband's hardness of heart, darkness had to flee. My face was in the face of God, not turned away from Him. The yoke was destroyed and I was released from the marriage. Like I said, darkness has to flee. I am repeating this because it is so important to clearly see that, "*It is a fearful thing to fall into the hands of the living God,*" (*Hebrews 10:31*); " *For Our God is a consuming fire,*" (*Hebrews 12:29*).

As for me, I am excited because what the enemy meant for evil God is turning around for my good. Praise the Lord! Nothing is too hard for him (*Jeremiah 32:27*).

In the spirit realm I am the head and not the tail. I am above and not beneath. I am blessed in the city and blessed in the country, blessed going in and blessed going out. I reach into God's realm, the realm of blessings and I draw out good things (*Deuteronomy 28:1-24*).

I take every thought captive unto the obedience of Jesus Christ, casting down every imagination, and every high and lofty thing that exalts itself against the knowledge of God (*2 Corinthians 10:5*).

No weapon that is formed against me shall prosper, but every tongue that rises against me in judgment, I shall show to be in the wrong (*Isaiah 54:17*).

I refuse to complain. I read *Romans 4:17* and I choose to speak the things that be not as though they were.

*Isaiah 48:15,17* tells me God teaches me to profit and leads me. Plus, according to *Ephesians 3:10*, God is able to do far more than I ever thought He could. I read the condition to the promises also. Consequently, I learned God calls me to participate prior to manifestation of the scriptures.

The list of promises from God is long, and I believe the Holy Spirit leads me to the verses I need when I need them. Then there is the importance of praise, worship, and prayer. I keep praying God will help me to be well balanced whether I am proclaiming the Word, singing, worshipping or praying. I learned it was most necessary for me to stay focused, to stay positive, and to speak words of life.

I tried not to be snared with the words of my mouth (*Proverbs 6:2*). There were plenty of people who spoke negatively about what I was going through, but I knew I had to stay positive. I wanted a positive harvest, not a negative harvest. I knew the Lord would not let me down. I trusted Him and knew that He would look after me, and He continues to look after me to this day. His track record is excellent and He doesn't change.

**The furnace is hot, very hot, but even in the furnace I am safe, protected, and able to actually rest in the loving arms of Jesus because He is carrying me. Praise the Lord. Sometimes there is only one set of footprints and sometimes there are two. Either way is fine with me. I never walk alone, that I do know.**

Now you know why I choose life. I choose the path of life in Christ Jesus. I choose to look in the realm of the Spirit of God and not be moved by circumstances. I am becoming more refined all the time as God purges me of impurities, as a refiner purges gold of dross (*Malachi 3:2-3*). Why? Because I yield; I want to become more purified, more brilliant as is a diamond.

Many people climb off the Master Potter's table when the going gets a bit rough, but they are the losers. Change is necessary and it is not God who needs to change, it is mankind. The more free I get, the more pliable I become in the hands of the Master Potter. I do not want to limit God in any way. I want no restrictions. Jesus Christ is Lord of my life, and that means He has control of every area. I really do trust Him and His plan for my life. My plans may be good, but for sure His are better. The smartest thing I ever did was simply step out of the way, and as I trusted Him, he fought the battles for me.

Remember, I did not pay for the divorce. My husband filed for divorce on the grounds of incompatibility, and he paid for the divorce. I did not pay for a lawyer. God is my attorney and it was God who vindicated me. It was God who provided for me. It was God who knew my needs and it is God who still performs miracles. So keep reading because I am fixin' to get one of the biggest miracles of my lifetime.

God is my Source and I give Him glory in advance! Meanwhile, I choose to STAY COOL! Even though the fiery furnace is very hot, I can stay cool as I remain "in Christ."

# 55. I SEE LAND

Jesus said, "*Come, walk with Me.*"
I turned and saw Him standing on the water
In obedience I stepped out in faith
Keeping my eyes on Jesus
Today, for the first time
I see land behind Jesus
That land is my land
That land is my country
That land is Canada
My Homeland

Heaven is my Hometown
Canada is my Homeland
Canada … here I come
Jesus called me back home
My family is calling me too
My heart is being prepared
Roots are being severed in Texas
As God leads me onward and upward

Knowing I am in the perfect will of God
Is what is important to me
More important than anything else
Jesus is first
Then my family
I look forward to building our relationship
I have much love to give

For God has given me much
He will prepare their hearts to receive
God used my son yesterday in a special way
He sent pictures online
Of the family at the lake for four days
The Canadian flag was waving proudly
And there was a photo of a huge anchor
Jesus is my Anchor, my Solid Rock

I don't know when I can move
But I will go ASAP
God will help me tie up loose ends here
God will provide for me
A home too
'Cause when it comes to blessing me
God is not through

He told me He would restore to me
All that was taken
I believe God and I will receive
God's got a plan
*Jeremiah 29:11* and *Romans 8:28* still work

So while I bask in the hot Texas sun
On this July 4th
And watch two horses approach the fence
Reaching for a drink of water
While the dog, "Patches," teases them
I choose to make the most of each day
Whether I am in Canada

Or
The USA
Glory To God

RONALD JONES

# 56. CANADA CALLING

IT WAS JESUS WHO SAID, *"COME,"* and that was two years earlier. First the prophetic word, then the manifestation of it … which seemed to be pretty close. How did I feel about that? It hurt to have Texas yanked from my heart because I had been in the United States nearly eleven years. It hurt a lot. Yet I was looking forward to spending time with my family, which had increased by four grandchildren since I went to Texas. Mixed emotions, but God healed and prepared.

All that mattered to me was that I be in the perfect will of God, whether in Texas or in Canada. I wanted to be where God wanted me. It did not matter where I wanted to be. I laid down my desires and meant it when I told God, *"Thy will be done,"* (*Matthew 26:42*).

So it was a whole new ballgame. My mind was remembering past memories of Canada, and I had the hope of more happy memories. Yet at the same time, I was feeling a tug as roots were severed there in Texas. It really was painful.

I loved Texas and the people so much, but when God calls, it is time to go. I asked Him to confirm by two witnesses (*Matthew 18:16*) that He was calling me back to Ontario and I believed He would soon. I also knew He would provide when it was time for me to make the move. He just asked me if I would go when He provided the funds. I agreed … with His grace.

It was July and I could see the American flag waving at me from my neighbor's porch. That part did not hurt. The Texas flag waving at me did hurt. It was more personal to me. Even though I had experienced many, many hurts in Texas, there had been good times as well, and good relationships too. However, it seemed this chapter of my life was coming to an end, and I found myself wondering if I would ever be able to come back. Only God knew at that point.

Some people have never had the privilege of traveling much or of living farther than a hundred miles from their birthplace. They may feel cheated. I can tell you pulling up roots from one country to another ... is not very comfortable. Perhaps it would have been less painful if I had felt there had been more successes during my time in Texas.

I can tell you that when I started writing this book I certainly had no idea all the turns these chapters would take. I just prayed God's purpose would be achieved.

The following poem was written for a very hospitable and gracious couple.

# 57. THE PATH OF BLESSING

Thank you
For being 'you'
For being vessels
Through which God flows
I can write these words
Because through y'all
I received
God knows

I was only one of many
That's been given hospitality
Whether it be meals, a room
Fellowship, a nap, transportation
You are 'Servants'
Of the Most High God
I've no doubt when it is time
Y'all will hear Jesus say, "WELL DONE"

God touched me from head to toe
When I rested in your 'Upper Room'
As I lay on the comfortable bed
It was as if slain in the Spirit an hour
I did not sleep but I knew
God was ministering to me
From deep within
With Holy Ghost power

Then I did have a nap
After which my mind was clear
The spiritual battle I'm in
Had recently been quite severe
That's why through y'all
I received what I needed.
God refreshed and healed and restored
As to Him I drew near

Spiritual surgery took place
In your beautiful home
While you were resting too
Nothing is too hard for God to do
He walked with me from room to room
As I enjoyed everything I saw
He reminded me
There's a lot more in Heaven too
I believe it and am not looking back

God used your beautiful home
To encourage me not to look back
He will restore all that was taken from me
Though my circumstances are bleak
My faith and courage are strong
God will do what He says He'll do
I'm sure you believe that too

I pray this little poem
Blesses both of you
It came from my heart
As a special *"Thank you."*

So be encouraged folks
Your labor is not in vain
Your ministry of love is appreciated

Lovingly
Linda Lou Jones

My dear friends, *John 13:14-17 NLT* says: *"And since I, your Lord and Teacher, have washed your feet, you ought to wash each other's feet. I have given you an example to follow. Do as I have done to you. I tell you the truth, slaves are not greater than their master. Nor is the messenger more important than the one who sends the message. Now that you know these things, God will bless you for doing them."*

Consequently, I KNOW why y'all are so blessed!!!

## Amarillo, TX GLORY TO GOD!
*Romans 8:28*

Praise God, I made it! I was in church. The pastor preached about crossing over into the Promised Land. I was one of many who went to the altar for prayer. I was so glad I obeyed the leading of the Lord. A spirit of abandonment no longer had a hold on me, nor did I have a broken heart.

I fell to the floor when God's power went through me. He set me free and bathed me in His love and peace. He gave me faith to believe that He would restore all that was taken from me. God proved Himself to be faithful, which you will see as you keep reading.

When I went back to my seat, a woman came and sat next to me. She asked if I had found a job yet. I told her I was writing this book but was not otherwise employed. She invited me to move into her home with her. I felt God's love and I knew that I knew this was where He wanted me to live for the time being and that it was His Divine timing.

The woman did not know that my divorce was final the next morning, but God knew. He put all the effects of *Romans 8:28* into action and met my every need as well. Someone else gave me a ride after church and offered to help me move. I recognized the hand of God. Healing received; delivered from fear, stress and torment; divorce final; crossing over; moving the same day; new open door—Praise God! Having favor with God and with man was great. God knows how to put things together. The pieces of the puzzle were falling into place. **God really can do a lot in a short time if we trust Him and don't get in His way.**

I am so thankful for the healing I received; as God opened deep wounds, I released forgiveness. He cleansed the wounds with the blood of Jesus, filled the wounds with His unconditional love, sealed them shut and made me stronger than ever before in each of those areas.

God did it. He knows when you really want to be free and your heart's desire is to have a pure heart, free of offense. It is the only way to walk in victory. I am not waiting until I get to Heaven to have victory. Jesus paid the price for me to have victory while on this earth. Praise the Lord!

God has given me wisdom and understanding as well as a strong desire to stay focused on Him, praise Him, be obedient, pray, study the Word, stay in an attitude of commitment and refuse to compromise. I do not gauge my progress by comparing myself with others in the congregation. Jesus is Who I go to when checking my spiritual growth. I do not want to be like most of the church because there is so much worldliness in the church. Not to offend anyone, but it has been appalling to me the number of Christians that have tried to get me to lower my standard. I am talking about church-attending Spirit-filled Christians.

Thank God He put the zeal in me to live a crucified life. There is no such thing as a padded cross. There will be suffering, but there is a Healer named Jesus Christ and He is closer to me and to you (if you have received him as your Savior) than the pain you are experiencing because He is in you.

I have learned that in every situation God's grace is sufficient (2 Corinthians 12:9). I am more and more free spiritually all the time, and I am staying free. It is a quality decision. Kind of like choosing to be an eagle for God, willing to make choices others are not making, and learning to soar in the spirit higher and higher above the storms to the tranquil area. It is wonderful!

I can honestly say I learned a great deal through those eleven years and two months. It was a very difficult time of my life, but I learned to forgive and not be bitter. I learned not to be concerned about my reputation when lies were told and I was slandered. I learned it is God I answer to and He sees my heart, so that is something I reminded myself of often.

I have total peace and continue to pray for the man who was my husband for eleven years. I pray he will learn to forgive, control anger, listen to God and obey, recognize his need to repent, and do things God's way. The wages of sin are death (Romans 6:23). I pray he will become a growing, committed Christian and be a disciple as he yields his will and gets free of pride because God has so much happiness for him, but only when his life is Christ-centered.

The flesh dies hard. It cannot be rebuked; it must be crucified. God will not force anyone to obey. He will not violate anyone's will. I prayed that God would not be limited and that my husband's lamp would not go out. "Once saved, always saved" is not scriptural. I pray his lamp will be full and he will be made whole in every way. I especially pray he will recognize his need for God's love in his heart and be able to release that love to others. I pray the same for his children and grandchildren (one of whom I had the joy of leading to the Lord). Our path has changed because, as the Word says, "Can two walk together, except they be agreed," (Amos 3:3)? God will not violate anyone's free will. He chose to walk away from God and from me. I chose to walk with Jesus and have no regrets.

I ask forgiveness for the pain I caused and I forgive my husband for everything. I forgive everyone who hurt me or betrayed me or treated me falsely. I do not hold anything against anyone. I choose to continue to focus on the Lord, press the computer keys and publish more books, songs and poems.

God will speak to hearts and bring hope, encouragement, gut-wrenching healing, salvation, deliverance—whatever it is that is needed—as He uses my books to expose darkness and set captives free. He did it for me and He can do it for you. He loves us too much to leave us the way we are. His Son, Jesus, is the answer. Only Jesus saves!

I pray this book is a blessing to each and every reader. God will give you the help and the direction you need. Trust Him completely and know that with God, *"all things are possible to him that believeth,"* (Mark 9:23)! Healing belongs to every believer.

Shadrach, Meshach, and Abednego, and Linda Lou, are out of the "fire!" Thank God! Not burned either, praise God! Thank you Heavenly Father for helping me, not giving up on me, and for inspiring me not to give up. I am so glad I am not a quitter because You aren't either. You are my example. *Jesus, I am so glad I squeezed Your hand so tightly!! It helped me a lot when You did NOT pull away! You led me through. All glory and honor goes to you, my Lord and Savior, Jesus Christ!*

This final chapter was completed less than twelve hours before the divorce was final. I had been writing the book for six months. I am so glad I did not withdraw and have a pity party for months or even years on end. I asked God to show me how He could have something good come out of all this mess because the Bible says that, *"with God all things are possible,"* (Matthew 19:26). **I believe He did it with this book. Nothing you go through is in vain when you give it to God. After all, He's the one that gets you through anyway. Hallelujah! Suffice to say, "IT IS FINISHED!"**

This book is a result of much purging of the dross and comes forth as purified gold to the glory of God. When I agreed to write it I asked the Lord to pierce through darkness and set souls free, set captives free, as they read the book. I also asked Him to see that the people who need this book get it. He is in charge of the marketing and distribution. The Holy Ghost put this book in your hands, and I pray you ask God if you are to read it again now. A second time through will prove very beneficial to each of you.

How do I know? Because I reread the book since writing it, and it proved to be very beneficial for me. That is when the Lord spoke and told me it will prove very beneficial to each of my readers too. I challenge you to do so and believe God will bless you accordingly.

**It is like the difference between praying … versus praying through.** God bless you as you do. But first read something that will really make you smile. It is the next chapter, and it is called, *From Reproach To A Red Letter Day*. I saved the best 'til last … well, almost last. There are a few more surprises coming.

# 58. FROM REPROACH TO A RED LETTER DAY!

SO THE DAY FINALLY ARRIVED THAT the divorce was finalized. God provided a ride to the courthouse so I could pick up a copy of the divorce papers filed by my husband. Total cost to me was exactly **$1.50!**

That is not a typing error; the cost was one dollar and fifty cents. I dare say I have favor with God! Praise the Lord because that is what it actually cost me for the divorce. Not many people can say that and I think it is worth repeating. Cost of the divorce was $1.50. I DO have favor with God!!

I can tell you I was thanking God I had the $1.50 because I had exactly $2.35 to my name. God met my financial need, but that is not all He did. He made something very beautiful out of that poignant day.

Read on about what happened when I was in the courthouse. It is the greatest blessing!!!!!

# 59. A SURPRISE FROM GOD

As I exited the county clerk's office
And entered a waiting room
I looked out the window
It was a sunny day
Temperature in the 80's
I looked up higher and said
*"Father, I never ever wanted*
*To bring reproach against You."*
My heart felt heavy, wrenched

He said
*"You do not have anyone's blood*
*On your hands."*
☺

That statement was worth more
Than anything money can buy
When it comes to unconditional love
God is just and God is love
*"There is therefore now no condemnation*
*to those which are in Christ Jesus,"* (Romans 8:1)

I said, *"Lord, all I wanted was a marriage*
*That would bring glory to You."*
He said, *"It did."*
I was shocked and asked, *"HOW?"*
He said, *"Through your book!"*

I was ecstatic!
When I left the elevator
My feet were on the ground
But my spirit was high
Even though transition is painful
I knew God had completed
Severing the soul ties and now
I could look forward
To a new beginning in Christ
Severing was over
The court would set a date
Anytime after the next twelve days
The divorce would be final
After eleven years of marriage

I marched down the sidewalk
With a skip in my step
I knew that I knew that I knew
That new doors were opening
The windows of heaven were open
And I was not walking alone

My Heavenly Father escorted me
With a skip in His step too
Time was passing quickly
And He's given me a job to do
Publish five books I've written
So I am focused and prepared
To answer His call

I have a vision from God
His presence is like
An eternally-lit lighthouse
Beckoning me at all times
Drawing me closer
Flooding me with peace and love
Every place I go

It is a new season now
Not just a new chapter
Perhaps even a new volume of books
As God stretches me a bit more
I finally reached the next phase of my life
And it is wonderful to know
I have no need to look back

When it is God's timing
A lot can happen in a short time
I will pray in the Spirit
And trust God to give me
Favor upon favor upon favor
That was prophesied on Sunday
I have sowed favor so I qualify
Just days later ... it manifested
Glory to God

It is an end of the tearing of roots
Thank God He got me through it
It is a new beginning for me now
Hallelujah

My Motto:
*"Small world, Big GOD!*
*To God Be The Glory. I'm Alive.*
*I AM ... A Walking Miracle!!!*

**AS FOR CLINT,**
**THE NEXT CHAPTER**
**Brings You**
**Up To Date.**

# 60. CLOSURE

Our eleven-year marriage ended in divorce, and I wrote this book to help others. Ten years have passed since the divorce, during which time Clint remarried. I stayed single. Then I received notice of Clint's passing. It was a shock even though we had been divorced ten years.

My first thought was, *"Lord, did he make it?!!!"* **No answer.** I asked again. Thoughts raced through my head because he had never repented to me, yet I did not want him in hell. It was a few days before the Lord confirmed His answer to me.

Meanwhile I soon learned that I had to walk out the grieving process even though we had been divorced ten years. That surprised me, and then God helped me see the big picture. When someone is part of your life for that long, there is a natural grieving process because not every day of the marriage was bad. Memories were triggered—good and bad—thoughts I did not want to think about, and my mind became a battleground indeed. The pain of those memories was gone, because I had forgiven and sought God for healing long ago.

Yet the memories were agonizing and the enemy wanted to torment my mind accordingly. The Holy Spirit ministered much love and understanding to me in the next few weeks. It was precious because I was alone and the few people I was in contact with showed surprise that I grieved at all. My help came not from people... but directly from my Master Mentor, the Holy Spirit! Special moments in His presence are the reason I emerged with healing complete. Since the funeral was 1600 miles away I also needed God's help to bring closure.

One day as I was reading my Bible, just days after Clint's death, five words leapt at me, *"....the dead are raised up,"* (*Matthew 11:5*). I had read that many times before, but never did it have the impact on me it did that day. The Holy

Spirit has a way of making it real, and He did. It's hard to explain; I just had a witness on the inside. So I then asked Him to confirm it, which meant I needed a second witness for it to become a confirmation *(Matthew 18:16)*.

One Sunday in church, the senior pastor was preaching and did not know about my prayer or of Clint's death. **In the midst of the preaching he spoke the very same five words I had read in *Matthew 11*. My heart leapt and the tears gushed forth.** Of all the words in the Bible, those five words were spoken from the pulpit and I knew that I knew ... God had just confirmed to me that Clint made it to heaven!! I was ecstatic!! That made it so much easier to bring closure.

As I sat in church that day, I prayed, *"Heavenly Father, thank you for helping me through this every step of the way. Thank you for revealing that Clint made it to heaven, and since I cannot talk to him, I need to pray this to help me bring closure. Please send an angel with this message from me to Clint."*

*"Hi Clint, Mission Accomplished, Congratulations! You made it to Heaven. God confirmed it to me and I am truly glad for you. I ask you to forgive me for any wrongdoing, any sin against you, and I know you will forgive me because there is no sin in heaven ... so thank you! I want you to know that I do forgive you for wrongdoing to me. It is over, done."*

*"God bless you and I sure hope when you see my parents that you have something good to say about me, eh!! I release you and let go now ... see you when it is my time to depart, but not yet because I am here doing this book and more, trying not to be jealous that you are dancing on streets of gold while I deal with all these terrible details, but I will get it done. God Bless You. Glad God kept you on the straight and narrow, as our song says. I pray this in Jesus' Name. Amen."* Then I prayed the angel deliver the message, and thanked the Lord for closure. Tears poured and incredible peace flooded my soul. It was finished. God did it. Closure.

I need to mention that while I did absolutely receive from God and I achieved closure, I caution my readers that it is not at all scriptural to speak with those that have died, **ever.** I received a release in my spirit from God to pray as I did. My prayer and message given to an angel was how the Holy Spirit taught me and it worked. The more I learn, the more I have to write about, because I write what I live. This keeps me inspired to be a learner.

So now, that season of his life and mine has closed. My focus is on my mission while on this earth now. Little did I know how God was about to liven up my days with a huge surprise.

One day I was speaking with a friend about Clint's passing. Long story short, she happens to live in Texas, as did Clint, and told me she thinks there is some money for me. I informed her that I was not his widow. He had been remarried for several years. We had been divorced for eleven years. She checked it out with an attorney friend and I was advised to look into it, as the laws in the United States are quite different from those in Canada.

So I did. First though, I sowed a seed of $58 and called forth a harvest. That means I gave an offering to God and planted it in good soil, as taught by Dr. Mike Murdock at The Wisdom Center in Texas. I applied his teaching of the Word of God by wrapping my seed in faith. Few teach the next step, but my testimony proves it works!

Next, I called forth this harvest: *"Father, I sow this seed wrapped in faith and call forth a harvest of You seeing* **that I get the amount of money You want me to have.** *Please oil the way with the Holy Spirit so it goes as smooth as silk and work out all the details because I don't even know who to phone. I also pray there will be no legal repercussion, in Jesus' Name. Amen."*

Then I made two phone calls to the US Government. I already had a social security number because I used to live in Texas, and that speeded up the application process. I mailed three legal documents to them, and in one week I received a phone call telling me how much my income was about to increase. It was a good thing I was sitting down because I learned that **my monthly income just DOUBLED, and that the new amount was going** to continue every month for the rest of my life! Glory to God. But that's not ALL!

A few weeks later I decided to phone again because I forgot to ask if it would take six months or more before I started receiving the money, since it was coming from the US government. At that point, I had lived in Canada for over a decade.

I phoned, and the man I spoke with got excited, then informed me that my application was approved that morning and had just been put on his desk! (**I said, *"Thank you Jesus."* That $58 seed was working!**) **No coincidences with God.** This man was in New York and I was in Ontario, Canada. My approved application arriving at the exact moment of my phone call was God's stamp of approval. I knew it!

Then I was told the money would be deposited into my account in about a week! But that's not all. I was told, **"You will be getting a LOT MORE THAN THAT!!!"** *"How?"* I asked. He answered, **"This is retroactive!"** I said, *"But he was alive!"* He said, **"That's the way we do it!"** (I wanted to say, *"Who am I to argue with the United States Government?"* but I didn't.) As I listened, he said, **"You need to open a bank account for US funds only. We will be depositing a lump sum of over $6,000 immediately into your account!!!"**

When I got off the phone I was crying. I knelt by my bed and started thanking the Lord. He spoke to me so clearly and said, **"Linda ... I Will <u>ALWAYS</u> Take Care Of You!"**

I will never forget His words or this miraculous provision, or the way the $58 seed smoothed the way. Within two weeks I had the lump sum, plus the lifetime income that is deposited each month, doubling my income. The world may say I am a senior living on a fixed income. Not my words. I say I am living under an open heaven and will continue to tithe and be obedient to God because I love Him and I love His surprises!! God honors obedience and will not be indebted to anyone.

The bottom line is that the qualifying factor for me to receive these funds was the fact that Clint and I were married ten years. That was the milestone that qualified me, according to the US government!

Now, after all the heartache, God was blessing me at a time when I needed the funds the most. He turned things around and favored me much. *Romans 8:28* is the scripture that hugs my heart because God surely does know how to have good come out of a situation if we trust Him, and I do.

**"Small World … Big GOD"** is still my motto! *Galatians 6:9, "Let us not be weary in well doing for in due season we shall reap if we faint not,"* is now my favorite scripture … understandably. I love seeing the hand of God at work in all areas of my life. Life is never dull. God won't lie, according to *Numbers 23:19.* My trust is in His flawless character.

Shadrach, Meshach, and Abednego made it safely out of the fiery furnace (*Daniel 3:27-28*), and so did I. I am not the same woman that entered the furnace, because the refiner's fire (*Malachi 3:2*) does change a person considerably. Hopefully I gained patience over the past ten years when I wanted to publish but had to trust God's timing. Now with this chapter I see why the ten-year delay. He truly does know how to put things together, so it is important not to lean to our own understanding (*Proverbs 3:5-6*) and get ahead of Him.

Thankfully I step out of the furnace as I bring this book to a close now, 2013, and emerge from the shadows with a New Beginning to the glory of God, *"with whom all things are possible,"* (*Matthew 19:26*).

Before I dedicate the final chapter, this book would not be in order if there were not an opportunity for prayer. If you are not saved, or are in a backslidden condition, I invite you to pray: "Heavenly Father, I ask you to forgive my sins, I repent. Jesus I accept you as my Savior and I ask you to be Lord of my life. Help me to know you personally and become more like you daily. Baptise me in the Holy Spirit with the evidence. I receive total forgiveness. I receive healing, deliverance from all evil, and I receive your joy. Thank you for loving me so much. Calvary was not in vain. I love you and I will serve you God. In Jesus' Name I pray. Amen.

If you prayed that prayer sincerely please send me a note: rightlady7@ gmail.com Thank you. Follow me on Twitter: https://www.twitter.com/ rightlady7

**FYI:** For your convenience, after the final chapter there is a Special 12 Point List on "**Abusive Relationships**".

**I Now Dedicate The Final Chapter To: "Clint", in his Honor.**

# 61. SHOW ME THE WAY TO GO

I WROTE THE FOLLOWING SONG ON my first trip with Clint in the 18-wheeler. I now realize that it is a "theme song" for the man who was my husband for over ten years. I insert it to honor his memory at this time.

## SHOW ME THE WAY TO GO
Show me the way to go, Oh Lord
Keep me on the straight and narrow
'Cause when I get through on this ol' earth
Heaven is where I want to go

Keep the wheels turning
I can't be late
Every load I must deliver
You know I need help from You, Oh Lord
You're the Abundant Life Giver (*John 10:10*)

Show me the way to go, Oh Lord
Keep me on the straight and narrow
'Cause when I get through on this ol' earth
Heaven is where I want to go … (*John 3:16*)
**CLINT Made It To Heaven**

**In 2011**

**MISSION ACCOMPLISHED**

**Glory To God!**

+++

As

For

Me:


I Am Loving Life

With Every Breath I Take

Because After Having Lung Surgery '02,

Every Breath I Take Is A Miracle!

I Am Ten Years

Totally

Cancer Free

Glory to God

Another Goliath Killed!

I Am Thrilled

To Publish This Book

And More Books Soon


*"WRITE ... From The Heart."*

Will Be Next

So Keep In Touch, eh!


**NEWS FLASH:**

**Guess Who Is Moving**

**From Canada**

**To TEXAS:**

**Me!!!**


**2013**

**Hallelujah**

**God Is Not Through**

## Blessing Me

☺

*Psalm 45:1 "... My tongue is the pen of a ready writer."*
### GLORY TO GOD

\*\*\*

. . . . . . . . . . . . . . . . . . . . . . . . . . . . . . . . . . . . . . . . . . . . . . . . . . . . . . . . .

## HUGE 'THANK YOU'
## To: DR. MIKE MURDOCK
### For The Following 12 Points

\*\*\*

## SPECIAL ADDITION

**Contribution Credits for Published Content:**
"Dr. Mike Murdock, Copyright 1995, The Making Of A Champion, Publishing Rights Owned By Wisdom International."
**Author:**
**Dr. Mike Murdock, Senior Pastor**
**The Wisdom Center**

**Dr. Mike Murdock, Author:**
**12 Point List On ABUSIVE RELATIONSHIPS:**

1. **Abandon Abusive Relationships With Those Who Subtract From Your Life.** "But the men that went up with him said, We be not able to go up against the people; for they are stronger than we. And they brought up an evil report of the land which they had searched unto the children of Israel,"(Numbers 13:31-32).

2. **Abandon Abusive Relationships With Those Who Do Not Discern Your Worth.** "Then Jesus said unto them, Take heed and beware of the leaven of the Pharisees and of the Sadducees,"(Matthew 16:6).

3. **Abandon Abusive Relationships With Those Who Kindle Strife.** "As coals are to burning coals, and wood to fire; so is a contentious man to kindle strife,"(Proverbs 26:21).

4. **Abandon Abusive Relationships With Those Who Do Not Increase You But Decrease You.** "Beware of the scribes, which desire to walk in long robes, and love greetings in the markets, and the highest seats in the synagogues, and the chief rooms at feasts,"(Luke 20:46).

5. **Abandon Abusive Relationships With Angry People.** "Make no friendship with an angry man; and with a furious man thou shalt

not go; Lest thou learn his ways, and get a snare to thy soul,"(Proverbs 22:24-25).

6. **Abandon Abusive Relationships With Those Who Create Stress In Your Life.** "And the land was not able to bear them, that they might dwell together: for their substance was great, so that they could not dwell together. And there was a strife between the herdmen of Abram's cattle and the herdmen of Lot's cattle,"(Genesis 13:6-7).

7. **Abandon Abusive Relationships With Those Who Weaken Your Passion For Your Assignment.** "Be not deceived: evil communications corrupt good manners,"(1Corinthians 15:33).

8. **Abandon Abusive Relationships With Those Who Will Hinder Your Future Success.** "And Abram said unto Lot, Let there be no strife, I pray thee, between me and thee, and between my herdmen and thy herdmen; for we be brethren. Is not the whole land before thee? separate thyself, I pray thee, from me: if thou wilt take the left hand, then I will go to the right; or if thou depart to the right hand, then I will go to the left,"(Genesis 13:8-9).

9. **Abandon Abusive Relationships With Those That Seek To Destroy The Divine Purpose of God In Your Life.** "But Peter said unto him, Thy money perish with thee, because thou hast thought that the gift of God may be purchased with money. Thou hast neither part nor lot in this matter: for thy heart is not right in the sight of God,"(Acts 8:20-21).

10. **Abandon Abusive Relationships With Those Who Do Not Respect your Dreams.** "And Joseph dreamed a dream, and he told it his brethren: and they hated him yet the more,"(Genesis 37:5).

**11. Abandon Abusive Relationships With Those Who Deceive You.** "And your father hath deceived me, and changed my wages ten times; but God suffered him not to hurt me,"(Genesis 31:7).

**12. Abusive Relationships With Those Who Do Not Share Your Beliefs And Convictions.** "For Demas hath forsaken me, having loved this present world, and is departed unto Thessalonica,"(2 Timothy 4:10).

www.ingramcontent.com/pod-product-compliance
Lightning Source LLC
Chambersburg PA
CBHW051815090426
42736CB00011B/1493

* 9 7 8 0 9 8 0 8 9 2 9 0 1 *